Dennis J. Cahill, MBA

Squeezing a New Service into a Crowded Market

"This book is a significant addition to what otherwise is an overcrowded field. By addressing the important topics of service from the perspective of the service itself, and not by the differences in products and services, the book is beneficial for both practitioners and students. The book focuses on introducing a new service into a market that already has multiple offerings supported by research, examples, and cases. It is perhaps these that make the book most appealing as readers can easily relate to the real world situations presented. Two of the most unique and interesting chapters are the ones on innovation and unconditional service guarantees, as material here is rarely dealt with in such a compelling way."

Robert D. Hisrich, PhD
*Professor and A. Malachi Mixon III
Chair in Entrepreneurial Studies,
Marketing and Policy Studies Dept.,
Case Western Reserve University*

"**E**ntrepreneurship. Market entry strategies. Creative service positioning. Winning. These are the recurring themes in Dennis Cahill's highly readable new book, *Squeezing a New Service into a Crowded Market*.

Cahill reviews many fundamental marketing principles that should be part of any sound marketing strategy: the marketing concept; positioning and mapping solutions; customer orientation; service guarantees; and innovation. But his treatment of these familiar subjects has a slightly different cadence from textbook treatments. He chats rather than lectures, and in a style which is breezy and informal.

The three service case studies are fun to read and help to illustrate several important points about marketing steps and missteps that are worth noting. He has gone to great lengths to support his statements and theories with references from the marketing and management literatures: the book includes an extensive bibliography. But, to his credit, this deference to academic writing does not interrupt the flow of his narrative.

If you are contemplating entering a crowded or mature market, I would recommend that you check out the lessons for success in Dennis Cahill's book."

W. Benoy Joseph, PhD
Chairman, Marketing Department, Cleveland State University

"**T**his is not your father's marketing book! Its very title is a trope; a marketing book about how to enter crowded markets is a book that must enter a crowded market of marketing books. With a post-modern wink of the eye, Cahill chooses to illustrate his topic by examples drawn exclusively from *failed* efforts in *publishing*, and he tackles doing so in an unconventional, fresh voice. He is not afraid to take a muscular stance in his own narrative.

To Cahill, all markets are crowded; the trick is to find an area that is somewhat overlooked. Similarly, he picks two *lenses* with which to view his case studies; one lens, the Marketing Concept itself, is so ubiquitous that we forget it's there until Cahill shows the penalties of doing so. The other lens is the powerful concept of perpetual mapping, which Cahill broadens to a sort of structural analysis tool instead of simply a statistical tool, showing its practical use as a thinking aid in everyday practice. We join the author on his tour of failed efforts, thoroughly enjoying the view.

If you're a marketer tired of the same few ways of dealing with marketing as a topic, you'll delight in this gem. For students interested in the actual practice of marketing, this should be a required reality check."

Steven Verba, BA
Chief Information Officer/
Senior Vice President,
Realty One Corporation,
Cleveland, Ohio

The Haworth Press, Inc.

Squeezing a New Service into a Crowded Market

HAWORTH Marketing Resources:
Innovations in Practice & Professional Services
William J. Winston, Senior Editor

New, Recent, and Forthcoming Titles:

Cases and Select Readings in Health Care Marketing edited by Robert E. Sweeney, Robert L. Berl, and William J. Winston

Marketing Planning Guide by Robert E. Stevens, David L. Loudon, and William E. Warren

Marketing for Churches and Ministries by Robert E. Stevens and David L. Loudon

The Clinician's Guide to Managed Mental Health Care by Norman Winegar

Framework for Market-Based Hospital Pricing Decisions by Shahram Heshmat

Professional Services Marketing: Strategy and Tactics by F. G. Crane

A Guide to Preparing Cost-Effective Press Releases by Robert H. Leoffler

How to Create Interest-Evoking, Sales-Inducing, Non-Irritating Advertising by Walter Weir

Market Analysis: Assessing Your Business Opportunities by Robert E. Stevens, Philip K. Sherwood, and J. Paul Dunn

Selling Without Confrontation by Jack Greening

Persuasive Advertising for Entrepreneurs and Small Business Owners: How to Create More Effective Sales Messages by Jay P. Granat

Marketing Mental Health Services to Managed Care by Norman Winegar and John L. Bistline

New Product Screening: A Step-Wise Approach by William C. Lesch and David Rupert

Church and Ministry Strategic Planning: From Concept to Success by R. Henry Migliore, Robert E. Stevens, and David L. Loudon

Business in Mexico: Managerial Behavior, Protocol, and Etiquette by Candace Bancroft McKinniss and Arthur A. Natella

Managed Service Restructuring–A Strategic Approach in a Competitive Environment by Robert L. Goldman and Sanjib K. Mukherjee

A Marketing Approach to Physician Recruitment by James Hacker, Don C. Dodson, and M. Thane Forthman

Marketing for CPAs, Accountants, and Tax Professionals edited by William J. Winston

Strategic Planning for Not-for-Profit Organizations by R. Henry Migliore, Robert E. Stevens, and David L. Loudon

Marketing Planning in a Total Quality Environment by Robert E. Linneman and John L. Stanton, Jr.

Managing Sales Professionals: The Reality of Profitability by Joseph P. Vaccaro

Squeezing a New Service into a Crowded Market by Dennis J. Cahill

Squeezing a New Service into a Crowded Market

Dennis J. Cahill, MBA

The Haworth Press
New York • London

The Haworth Press, Inc., 10 Alice Street, Binghamton, NY 13904-1580

Library of Congress Cataloging-in-Publication Data

Cahill, Dennis J.
    Squeezing a new service into a crowded market / Dennis J. Cahill.
        p.   cm.
    Includes bibliographical references and index.
    ISBN 1-56024-939-0
    1. Service industries–Marketing. I. Title.
HD9980.5.C34 1994
658.8–dc20   94-45865
                                                                                                        CIP

To my parents,
Lois G. and Kevin J. Cahill,
with a lifetime of love.

ABOUT THE AUTHOR

Dennis J. Cahill, MBA, MA, has headed North Union Associates, Inc., a finance, investment, and marketing consulting firm in Cleveland, Ohio, since 1983. He founded the firm after almost a decade of increasingly responsible financial positions held in the cement and banking industries. Mr. Cahill has also taught undergraduate and graduate marketing and finance courses at three Cleveland area colleges. He has published numerous articles in scholarly and professional publications and has spoken at national professional conferences and local meetings. In October, 1992, he was appointed editor of the *Journal of Product and Brand Management*. While heading North Union Associates, Mr. Cahill has been active in many aspects of new product and new service development, from initial concept through delivery of completed product to end user. He is a member of the American Marketing Association, the Academy of Management, the Association of Psychological Type, and the Association for Consumer Research.

CONTENTS

PART III. CONCLUSIONS AND IMPLICATIONS

Foreword

Many people are attempting to examine the nature of service enterprises these days. Far too many are approaching this subject by looking at the differences between goods and services rather than simply exploring the nature of the product. Dennis Cahill has, with examples, simply looked at services from the perspective of customer design and internal development. In so doing, he avoids the many pitfalls that emanate from the more prevalent approach.

After many years of conversation with Dennis, I can say that reading this book is quite like spending a long evening exploring a topic–always witty, full of opinions, sharp observation, and most important, a stimulant to thoughts of one's own. What this book does more than anything is present a point of view, supported by research, experience, and examples, that enlightens and enlarges everyone's thinking about the way they pursue their business.

Business owners and managers can read this with immediate profit. Anyone who intends to give seminars and assistance to small service enterprises ought to read it. Besides its intellectual content, this book is enjoyable to read–it does not feel like work. Yet, unlike a great deal of business-related reading, you find yourself thinking about what was said long after you have put it down.

Dennis is a friend, but even if I disliked him, I would have enjoyed this book. Have fun and read for profit.

Sharon V. Thach
Associate Professor
Tennessee State University
Nashville, TN

Preface

This is a work that is intended both for practitioners of the art of services marketing and for advanced marketing students interested in "real-world" applications of some of the marketing theories to which they have been exposed. This work attempts to meet the important challenge of how to squeeze another service offering into what appears to be an already crowded marketplace. Is there room for another law firm? Another hospital? Another newspaper? Another spreadsheet program?

One way to answer this question is to enter the market and find out. Perhaps the new entrant can outspend the existing offerings, or utilize more creative advertising and promotion, or through other means elbow the existing offerings aside and perhaps gain enough market share from some or all of them to survive–or even to attain supremacy. International Business Machines did this when it entered the personal computer market in the early 1980s; most of the competitors who so filled the market have since gone out of business. Yet a better way to find an answer is to perform various kinds of research to determine if the market would welcome the new offerings and at what price(s) it will accept them.

Part I of this book explores the research necessary to utilize the better approach mentioned above. Chapter 1 outlines methods to use for determining just how crowded the market really is; often, it only seems crowded. Further, it sometimes pays not to be the first into a market. Chapter 2 defines the Marketing Concept and applies it to a new product case. Chapter 3 discusses perceptual mapping, a research concept with great potential for practical application in squeezing new offerings into what seems at first blush to be a crowded marketplace. It may in fact be a marketplace that simply has a lot of offerings in it–not necessarily the same thing.

Part II presents three detailed case examples from my files of the ways in which various services were offered to crowded markets–

and failed. The case analyses will dissect the failures, explain where, why, and how they failed, and interpose what could and *should* have been done to prevent–or at least reduce the probability and cost of–failure. As both a practitioner and a teacher, I prefer to analyze failures. Success occurs for many reasons, but failure usually has one or two very clear causes. Every client wishes to be thought of as *sui generis,* but the analyses in Part II will show there is a common thread running through these failures.

Part III will deal with innovation and how to handle it in a service firm. We all want innovation and profess that only innovative services and programs will provide future growth for our firms and our economy. Nevertheless, a firm that innovates at the expense of its core business(es)–a not-uncommon phenomenon–may run into trouble quickly. Perhaps the IBM experience mentioned above–allowing others to develop the market and then stepping in when it looks to be long lasting–can work for other firms; it surely is a lower-cost/lower-risk approach than pioneering, even though research continues to show that the pioneering firm derives superior returns. (See Alpert, 1987, for a review of this research.)

Although there has not been a tremendous amount written on new services development–certainly not when that subject is contrasted to the voluminous writings on new product development–there has been some that rates a mention. One article in particular has listed sixteen hypotheses for academics to test (Fugate and Turley, 1992)–see Table A. Although I will not directly address these hypotheses, and this is not a research book, my thoughts on these will become evident as the reader proceeds through the book.

Any author has too many debts to acknowledge individually. Often we stand on the shoulders of giants, which makes it easy to see farther than even the giants. In my case there are no apparent giants, simply a lot of ordinary-sized people who have helped my intellectual development through the years. Nevertheless, standing on their shoulders has enabled me to see much farther. Specifically, several individuals must be mentioned by name for help with the present work. Dr. Sharon Thach read much of this work and its initial material, as did Robert M. Warshawsky; both offered many comments, some of which I have heeded and all of which I have considered. Bill Gunlocke, former publisher of the Cleveland *Edi-*

tion, and Hal Douthit graciously allowed me access to material on their publications. Further, Hal Douthit has contributed material on other ventures and products and provided consulting jobs from time to time which have made working on this book easier.

Editors and anonymous reviewers of several journals need to be thanked for their comments on papers and articles which were earlier forms of some of the material presented herein, some of which were published, some of which were not. All the comments were valuable: *Journal of Consumer Marketing, International Journal of Research in Marketing, Journal of Consumer Research, Pricing: Strategy and Practice, Academy of Management Journal, Marketing News, Services Marketing Today, Journal of Marketing, Environment and Behavior, Journal of Business-to-Business Marketing, Journal of Professional Services Marketing, Journal of Customer Service in Marketing and Management, Journal of Business and Industrial Marketing, Journal of Services Marketing,* and the *Journal of Product Innovation Marketing.* Reviewers of the late Services Marketing Conference of the American Marketing Association, the High-Technology Management Conference of the University of Colorado, and the Small-Business Institute Directors Association Conference also offered comments on several papers.

Finally–but, of course, *never* finally–thanks to my wife Jeanine and children Abigail and Teddy for understanding when I was abstracted or missing.

TABLE A. New Service Hypotheses

1. Since services are intangible, the new services development model requires more stages than the new product development model.
2. Due to differences in market conditions and regulations, different service industries will emphasize different stages in the new service development process.
3. Service firms do not use a formal new service development process for all new services added to their service mix.
4. Smaller service firms are less likely to go through a formal new service development process than are larger service firms.
5. Business strategies and new service strategies are not usually developed by most service firms.
6. Business strategies and new service strategies are more likely to be developed by larger service firms than they are by smaller ones.
7. Employees are a useful source of new service ideas for both small and large service firms.
8. Many service firms do not have a formal new service development process and imitate competitor's products.
9. Larger service firms are more likely to blueprint new services than are smaller service companies.
10. The new service concept will not be well developed until fairly late into the process.
11. There is no consensus on what constitutes sound business analysis for new services.
12. Because of their unique characteristics, services have more external validity problems during development and testing than do products.
13. Most service firms use covert, abbreviated, or accelerated test marketing.
14. Market testing is more likely to be used by service firms with multiple sites.
15. Lower levels of formal service development result in higher levels of new service failure.
16. Failure rates for new services are higher than they are for new products.

Source: Fugate, Douglas L. and Turley, L. W. "The New Service Development Process: An Assessment," published in Victoria L. Crittenden, ed. *Developments in Marketing Science*, xv, ©1992. Reprinted with permission of publisher.

PART I.
RESEARCH

Chapter 1

How Crowded Is the Market?

How crowded is the market? By definition, all markets at all times are crowded. In the 20-plus years that I have been involved with business since I started on my MBA at Cleveland State University in the early 1970s, I have never seen a market that was less-than-abounding with offerings. Sometimes it may be a stretch to realize that the market exists, much less that it is crowded. But, then, that is the essence of Levitt's "Marketing Myopia" (1960)–one needs to define one's market rather broadly. The mere fact that few people had ever heard of a personal computer in 1975 did not mean that there was a void; people who would be using personal computers daily in the 1990s were using calculators, either programmable or not, in 1975. In 1970, these same people were using Comptometers or slide rules. Prior to the invention of either, scratch paper and pencils served the same function. Therefore, every introduction becomes a case of trying to "squeeze" the new into a crowded market. There are always products or services which can be–and, at the beginning, are–substituted for the new item.

If this is true for products–and I think that the evidence is fairly clear that it is–citation of more examples beyond the personal computer should not be necessary–is it true for services? I worked in the Corporate Trust Department at Central National Bank of Cleveland from 1978 to 1982. During that time the banking industry in general underwent astonishing changes in the numbers and kinds of deposit vehicles that institutions were able to offer their customers. True "money-market" checking accounts became available to bank customers nationwide, allowing people to earn interest on their checking deposits, and variable interest-rate deposits were offered by most banks, to name only two new vehicles. And yet, not only did banks have to shove these two choices into what was a crowded market–competing financial intermediaries had already offered these instruments to their customers–but these investments had to compete with the myriad offerings that the banks made themselves. Unable because of regulation to offer true interest-bearing checking accounts, banks had made zero-balance accounts paired with a savings account available to their favored customers long before, offering the essence of interest-bearing checking accounts without the structure of one.

Further, even in the Corporate Trust Division itself there were changes during the years I was there that show how crowded a market can be. Prior to my employment, Central National had earned a reputation for being out of the Indenture Trusteeship business. This was an untrue reputation but no one in Corporate Trust much cared until I showed up and realized that this was a line of business that offered significant enhancements to the "preferred" business of Employee Benefit Trust accounts. In the three years during which I tried to sell the service to firms who would be interested, I was continually faced with the challenge of convincing potential clients that we were in fact in the business and could do at least as good a job as the competing banks in Cleveland.

Dholakia and Venkatraman (1993) discuss another kind of market that is, almost by definition, always crowded: services that compete with products. In fact, in the example which leads off their article–how does one see a movie?–the product (a videocassette to be viewed at home) can be either a pure product–a cassette purchased by the consumer–or a hybrid–a cassette rented by the consumer for one-time viewing at home–or a pure service–a movie watched on television, either through a cable service or "over-the-air" without cable. Dholakia and Venkatraman state that in this kind of market the problem for the marketer is first to create generic demand–watching movies in theaters–and then to focus that demand on a specific provider. Services have a higher chance of dominating over a product when the benefits they offer are not easily duplicated in a tangible form. In the example of watching movies, it is clearly home-viewing which has triumphed in the 1990s; in other markets the triumph of products is not so clear.

How much more crowded can a market get? I suppose that a more crowded market is the market for stocks, particularly, in the early 1990s at least, the market for new equity (the Initial Public Offering market). Lehman Brothers advertised in *The Wall Street Journal* of January 13, 1994 (page C17), under a picture of an airport with a control tower, two air traffic controllers, and seven planes in sight, as follows:

> Issuing Equity in a crowded field requires a partner with a sense of timing. Market conditions for issuing stock are more favorable than they have been in years, with the number of companies in the queue growing every day. In this crowded environment, issuers need an experienced partner to help them gain access to every market and every type of investor the world over. . . . As a leading global underwriter, Lehman Brothers has raised over $18 billion of equity capital for our clients in the past 2 years. What is far more important than the dollar figure, however, is the depth of experience represented by that figure. . . . This is precisely the sort of vision that's necessary when attempting to land safely in a crowded field. . . .

Thus, Lehman shows a doubly crowded market. The market for new equity issues is crowded, but so is the market for underwriters, as there are literally dozens of firms who underwrite new equity issues.

How about a service that "creates its own market," analogous to the personal computer cited above? The quintessential service which created its own market must be Federal Express. The story of the company is so well known that I will not repeat it here. What I will discuss is the fact that even Federal Express entered a crowded market.

How can a firm which is generally credited with *creating* its market have entered a crowded market? First, remember that overnighting important packages is nothing new. Intracity packages have been courier-delivered since time immemorial. Intercity *messages* have been sent by telegraph for more than 150 years. Intercity packages of either great value or great importance have been sent overnight (or faster) for at least half a century. It has been possible for that long to buy a plane or train ticket, give the package to an employee, get that employee to the terminal, and have the employee deliver the package at the other end. And if the package was too cumbersome or heavy for a courier, air freight was long available. Or if packages were sent very often, a private network of small planes could take them across the country; the Federal Reserve Board has long had its own "Air Force" of small planes which fly from Federal Reserve Bank to Federal Reserve Bank carrying checks for clearance.

All this was possible, but expensive. And because of the expense, it was rarely done. And because of the expense, people only infrequently thought that their package was important enough to require the trouble and expense to send it by courier. The genius of Fred Smith was that he caught a wave of changing time-perception. More and more people were willing to think that their work was important enough to warrant overnight shipping if it only cost a few dollars rather than a few hundred, especially if the shipping service could be differentiated from the loathed Postal Service.

Along comes Fred Smith with his idea to fill the night skies with airplanes carrying hundreds and thousands of small packages–basically mail–for delivery the next day. Easily and smoothly. Or in the words of an early Federal Express television commercial: "So simple that even the Chairman can do it." Federal Express soon became the generic word for sending something overnight–"FedEx it." Federal Express quickly became the preferred way to send mail; I know of instances where mail was sent crosstown in Cleveland by Federal Express via Memphis, Tennessee, rather than trust delivery to the Postal Service. This was in essence a replication of the dozens of express companies which handled small-package freight in the nineteenth century taking money home from Union soldiers at the front during the Civil War; the Post Office has long been distrusted in this country.

Although Federal Express's success came neither overnight nor without a protracted effort, an effort which gobbled up several infusions of venture capital before turning a profit, in a sense it was an acting-out of Levitt's "Marketing Myopia." The Post Office saw itself as a monopoly provider of first class mail service at a low price for a delivery time that was elastic. United Parcel Service delivered packages more quickly and at a higher price than the Post

Office, but not overnight. Air freight could deliver goods overnight, but not "So simple that even the Chairman can do it"; the documentation needed was confusing to complete. No one offered a quick, easy, relatively inexpensive way to get small packages delivered overnight. There was a gap in the market offerings that allowed Federal Express to slip in to compete with two very large competitors: United Parcel Service and the Federal Government. And to win. Federal Express's success forced both UPS and the Postal Service to begin offering equivalent services in an attempt to regain market share. The market that Federal Express created is once again crowded with their direct competitors, but on the terms that Federal Express defined.

If markets are always crowded, why bother to innovate, like Federal Express? There are two kinds of "crowdedness" which should be clear from the above discussion. The first is a crowdedness caused by the fact that there are always substitutes available, even for the seemingly unique product or service. The second is the follow-on crowdedness caused by the successful introduction of a new product or service; "me-too" goods and services will pour into a market successfully developed by the pioneer, as UPS and the Postal Service (and numerous other firms) started their own overnight delivery services. This book shows how to deal with the former kind of crowdedness. The latter is mitigated by two facts.

First is the fact that research shows that the pioneer in a market derives superior returns and market share over later entrants. Robinson and Fornell (1985) claim that the higher market shares of pioneers seem to be derived from both firm-based superiority as well as customer-information advantages–the name recognition that comes with being the firm that defines the market. Carpenter and Nakamoto (1988) state that the pioneer brand is close to the definition of the category because "category ideals are derived from experience with the pioneer." By default, the most frequently experienced brand will be the pioneer, and as such it provides a cognitive reference point, its name becoming synonymous with the category–like Federal Express. Lawless and Fisher (1990) discuss "nonimitability" in their article on sources of competitive advantage in new products. They list seven product components which affect nonimitability: form, function, intangibles, pricing, promotion, distribution, and firm characteristics. Being first matters, even though there is strong anecdotal evidence, particularly from the high-tech world, that it is not the only criterion which determines durable competitive advantage and profitability. IBM illustrated this by coming into the personal computer market after Apple had developed it and then dominating that market. Further, Lotus 1,2,3 successfuly entered the spreadsheet market long after VisiCalc succeeded in defining the market (although this is a special case, perhaps, because Lotus's success was aided by the squabble between VisiCalc's publisher and the firm which sold the program) and took it over showing that in at least some markets the "advantage" is merely a head start in a never-ending race. Thus, although it is undoubtedly true that pioneers enjoy advantages, they probably are not permanent and should not be viewed as such.

The second mitigating factor in "me-too" crowdedness follows from the first. If the pioneer enjoys the advantage of a larger market share than later entrants–for however long–it follows that the more the *market* is expanded, the more sales the share-leader will garner. It is perhaps apocryphal that the ads featuring the pink Everready battery bunny in the early 1990s also raised sales for its larger competitor Duracell; nevertheless, that danger always exists for a second-place share firm. This fact is one of the reasons why it is often difficult to displace the market leader. All marketing expenditures need to be larger for the smaller-share firms. Since they are allocated over a (by definition) smaller number of units sold, marketing costs per unit would then be higher for the smaller firms, making it more difficult for them to be lower-cost producers, thus making it awkward for them to sell at lower prices than the leader.

How realistic are these two facts–pioneer advantages and cost advantages–for *service* firms? Although there is little research available on the advantages which accrue to service pioneers, the research from product pioneership is so compelling that I feel that service pioneership must follow the same path, although perhaps not to the same extent as products (but my suspicion is that it is as least as important). Since reputation is so important in services (more about this later), being first into a market and thus defining the market and the service allows a firm to set the reputation level for the service and the market. Lower marketing costs are possibly less important in services than in products, as so much of services marketing is not cost-driven nor suitable to the wiles of the cost accountants.

So–where are we? If we have to be first into a market to be durably successful, how can I in good conscience entitle this book *How to Squeeze a New Service into a Crowded Market?* The preceding pages almost define this process of squeezing a new service into a crowded market as not worth the effort. The necessary strategy is to define one's market so that one is *not* trying to squeeze into a crowded market, but rather to find a market–or a part of the market–that is not being served by the current market offerings and design the new service to thus be the first into this part of the market. Although the market will be crowded because substitutes are being used–like the Federal Express example cited above–if done successfully the new service will define a new market, becoming the pioneer entrant which all other providers will have to chase.

How can this be done? There are two tools which should prove quite helpful. The first is more a mindset than a technique: the Marketing Concept, which describes how to think about one's offerings. The second is a technique known as perceptual mapping which can help analyze gaps in the services being offered by competitors (and oneself, for that matter) and allows a firm to tailor the new service with attributes that customers want that are either not being currently offered or, perhaps, not being currently promoted.

Chapter 2

The Marketing Concept

The Marketing Concept is not new. It is now more than 35 years since John McKitterick (1957) put forth the idea of the Marketing Concept: meeting customer needs as a philosophy of business. In the ensuing years, while there has been profound debate on the idea, the *concept* has survived. A recent undergraduate marketing text chosen at random devotes two pages of explanation and a chart to the Marketing Concept describing it–with little change from McKitterick–as a "customer-oriented, integrated, goal-oriented philosophy for a firm, institution, or person" (Evans and Berman, 1987).

One would expect that any concept basic enough to appear in an introductory textbook would be wholeheartedly subscribed to by practitioners and academics alike. In the case of the Marketing Concept, however, nothing could be further from the truth. Again, to sample my files at random, Hirschman (1983) proposes that the concept is not applicable to artists and ideologists because of "the personal values and social norms that characterize the production process" of these persons' output; this fact may explain why artists starve–the Marketing Concept is, of course, rooted in the marketplace. Hampton and Lane (1982) state that the Marketing Concept is anathema to at least a large portion of the employees in the newspaper industry–those on the editorial side (more about this fact later). And recently, Brown (1992) has denied the applicability of the Marketing Concept in High Technology products. Yet Peters and Waterman (1982) forced American business to focus on their customers. Crawford (1983) states that the Marketing Concept "appears to be an impossible philosophy to put into effect. . . . [It] is still loudly proclaimed but seldom seen. It represents the unattainable–the marketing utopia."

Dick Berry (1988), in an article aimed at practitioners, states that the Marketing Concept "will continue to gain in importance and application." He continues that if he were given the opportunity to rewrite the Marketing Concept he would consider adding the following dimensions: "emphasizing segmentation, niching, targeting, customer service support and value-added in the exchange process, stressing the delivery of customer satisfaction." The Marketing Concept is "setting goals, not making a mad dash for profits."

Despite the intuitive appeal of the Marketing Concept, there has been almost complete resistance to a customer-need orientation as an organizing principle for new product development and marketing in high technology. This is especially true in the field of personal-computer software. A cursory reading of trade weeklies that cross my desk shows a recurrence of themes: users are ignorant; users do not know what they want; new products must be developed by engineer *savants* and then exposed to the unwashed. It is as though the work by von Hippel (1986) and Herstatt and von Hippel (1992) on new product ideas did not exist, or that Taylor (1977) had not made the perceptive suggestion that new product development should be conducted among heavy users of the product-class, rather than among general users. Since general users are more likely to be early triers, their reaction to the new product will be critical to its success because of their potential sales volume. There is a story, possibly apocryphal, about a peripheral manufacturer who surveyed possible OEM (original equipment manufacturers) customers about what their specifications would be for a particular peripheral; armed with these specifications, the manufacturer set out to exceed those specifications which seemed most important to the customers and only meet those which seemed least important–with great pecuniary success. Similarly, *The Wall Street Journal* (Gupta, 1993) reported that Biosite Diagnostics, Inc., a biotech start-up, used costly market research to show investors that there was a demand for its technology–albeit in a relatively small market–leading to quick success for the firm. As far back as the late 1970s Merle Crawford (1977) was criticizing product developers and market researchers for the lack of a meaningful role for market research in the product-development process, leading to high new-product failure rates.

To a certain extent this emphasis on the Marketing Concept pits me against some of the Product Development literature which emphasizes some objectively determinable product superiority as the criterion which most distinguishes new product successes from failures. One often hears this position from engineers. Good examples of those who fall closer to the "product-superiority" end of the spectrum than I are Cooper and Kleinschmidt (1987, 1993), Cooper (1979, 1986, 1993), Calantone and Cooper (1977), Cooper and de Brentanis (1991), and Kleinschmidt and Cooper (1991). Although willing to admit that it may take a superior product to win market acceptance, product superiority does not guarantee acceptance; further, it is possible to gain market acceptance with a less-than-superior product which is marketed effectively, particularly if the marketplace does not *want* "superiority" on the particular dimension or does not perceive that the product is inferior.

The original version of Lotus 1,2,3 is a good example of a product that had little if any "objective" superiority when introduced; it was, however, well marketed and entered the marketplace at a time when its competition–VisiCalc–was having organizational difficulties. One path out of my seeming opposition to the above-cited literature is to state the problem a bit differently, placing another twist on the argument. If one defines "superior product" to mean one that best meets *customer-defined* needs and not as something defined by a supposed technical expert, there is no distinction between the literature and my position.

I have often heard, "It is impossible to ask consumers what they want in high tech." One observer stated that if, ". . . as is the case of many innovations, no market exists, and if potential customers are unable adequately to understand the product, then market research can provide only negative answers" (Brown, 1992). Although this statement may be self-evident (and possibly true for packaged goods), behind it lurks terrible danger to any firm, particularly one trying to introduce a highly sophisticated new product or innovative service.

"Often the problem with a new product is not that it fails to perform well but that it offers no significant advantage to the user. Many new products have failed because manufacturers could perceive product differences, but customers could not" (Evans and

Sherman, 1979:296). Saving nanoseconds of processor time is an issue to engineers and programmers (and to product reviewers), but many users cannot perceive how this press for speed helps them. However, if a program can perform many word-processing tasks simultaneously, or–based upon previous work performed–in an "expert-system" process, it could prove to be a great benefit and could propel me to purchase a new, expensive, and much faster machine. Otherwise, saving nanoseconds through faster processor speed makes no sense to me since most of my computer time is spent word-processing, a notoriously bad use of faster processors. I am a 35-word-per-minute touch-typist; a faster computer chip will not speed up my typing. (See Cahill and Warshawsky, 1993, for further development of this line of thinking, and Higgins and Shanklin, 1992, for its counterargument.) As Morris and Lundstrom (1984:228) put it, too often the assessment of customer needs is "based upon questioning and not analysis. That is, obtaining representative reaction, but not analyzing the underlying causes and implications of such reactions."

The greatest danger to marketers of ignoring the Marketing Concept is that so few products or services are innovations. Microcomputers date from the mid-1970s; even the IBM PC is over ten years old. Microwave ovens are more than 25 years old. Burglar alarm systems have been with us for more than 20 years. Residential solar heat has been passé for more than a decade. The lack of consideration of the Marketing Concept cannot be laid on the doorstep of product innovation. Rather it is in the Mandarin's sneer–so evident in the statement about marketing quoted above–that "we know what products to design, and you will buy what we think you should have." This sneer is a recipe for bankruptcy, particularly when trying to squeeze a new service into a crowded market. It can lead a firm to lose all sense of proportion, and throw good money after bad. In a list of lessons about the new product development process, Marquis (1976) lists as Lesson #2: Recognition of demand is a more frequent factor in successful innovation than recognition of technical potential.

I would like to introduce the contrasting tales of two products developed by a client of mine: the *CompuAd* family of computer programs and *AutoAd*. (See Cahill, Thach, and Warshawsky, 1994, for details.) These tales serve as an example of how a firm can lose its sense of proportion and press on to develop a product for which there seems to be no willing market, and to what uses the Marketing Concept can be put to prevent the firm's continuing to throw good money after bad, year after year.

In 1977, DECOY, Inc. (not the firm's real name) began the development of *CompuAd,* a computer program to write classified advertisements for houses. *CompuAd* was born over lunch when the Chairman asked a programmer if he could design a program to write those advertisements. DECOY folklore states that the motivation came from the bad advertisements delivered to DECOY publications by real estate agents. (This motivation–attempting to write "better" advertising copy by computer–is not confined to real estate classified advertisements; Burke, Rangaswamy, Wind, and Eliashberg [1988] report on "AdCAD," a computer program developed to write general advertising copy. The results they show are provocative, to say the least. And Bulkeley [1994] reports on *SportsWriter,* a program for writing football and basketball stories for small town weekly newspapers; he reports that the main complaint seems to be that, although the writing is not bad, the *reporting* is all but nonexistent.) By the late 1980s, several hundred copies of *CompuAd* and its progeny had been sold in the United States and overseas. The program's design team worked continually on improving the basic operation of *CompuAd* in two major respects. The first was to get the program to write "better" ads; better was defined as what a good copywriter would produce from a given set of features–"engineeringly" better. The second was the on-going drive to produce these results faster.

By February, 1984, *CompuAd* was being used in a few sites, mostly DECOY publications. The program was now being run on a minicomputer owned by DECOY. Any buyer would need to make a major investment in equipment to run the program. The package was a major investment by DECOY, but had paid almost no return. The Chairman was unhappy and, at this juncture, I was brought in as a marketing consultant.

DECOY management spent much of 1984 reviewing the situation and, in February, 1985, decided to convert *CompuAd* to a personal computer program to be sold at retail. DECOY personnel spent most of 1985 changing the program to the new format. Much time was spent in trying to fit the program into the "standard" IBM PC of the time, with only 256 kilobytes of memory. This attempt was unsuccessful, but a new stripped-down PC version of *CompuAd*–called *NewsAd*–emerged.

All this work took place against a November 1985, deadline: The National Association of Realtors Annual Convention and Trade Show in New Orleans. The team spent the summer of 1985 frantically designing the package and writing the manual and marketing copy for a program whose final configuration had not been decided upon. *NewsAd* Version 1.0 made its debut, on time, at a price of $225. Although DECOY sold only 40 packages at the show, the company distributed much collateral material, obtained numerous sales leads, and learned from real estate agents what they wanted in the product's second release.

DECOY personnel left New Orleans convinced that, with a little more work, *NewsAd* would become a big seller. Some routines that had been excised from *CompuAd* in the rush to get *NewsAd* ready and slimmed down to 256K would have to be squeezed back in; this fact was clear from discussions with people on the Show floor. Nevertheless, everything seemed to point to a success for the product; many agents seemed excited about the concept of using a computer to write their advertisements. (See Exhibit 2.1 for an example of an advertisement written by the original *CompuAd*. This

EXHIBIT 2.1

CEO FANTASY HOME

Pillared stone Colonial close to lovely park. Remodeled, on 18 acres, only one owner. 18 Fireplaces, master suite, modern kitchen, 12 BR/12 Baths, pantry, finished basement, swimming pool. PLUS *Near bus *Vaulted ceiling *Foyer *Easy commute *Slate roof *Formal dining room *Garden *Servants' quarters *Bookcased library *Double entry doors.

$30,000,000

advertisement was written many years ago based upon data supplied by the White House staff; it has been used as a sample of *CompuAd*'s capabilities and as advertising copy–always with good results from readers.)

Still, sales did not materialize. The conclusion was reached by the Chairman that real estate agents were not buying *NewsAd* because they were afraid of computers and thus did not have them in their offices. DECOY would have to develop and market stand-alone machines dedicated to running *CompuAd*. No research went into this conclusion; it was an intuitive insight. The Chairman has frequently had such intuitive insights which have paid off handsomely; this one was to prove wrong. DECOY embarked on creating the *AdWriter,* the stand-alone, dedicated *CompuAd* machine.

In early 1987, three different prototypes of the *AdWriter* were shown at a gathering of DECOY's customers in hopes of obtaining good feedback from them as to design and features. Unfortunately, the customers were asked only one question: Which physical appearance did they prefer? The customers spent very little time with the machines and had no opportunity to use the *AdWriter* to actually write sample ads. Worse, these individuals were executives in their firms–they no longer needed to produce ads for houses. Yet design decisions were made based upon the casual remarks, often directed by DECOY personnel, of these few individuals. Ultimately, work went for naught as DECOY decided to use a commercially available computer with an *AdWriter* nameplate rather than enter into manufacturing the machines itself. One year and tens of thousands of dollars were wasted on manufacturing a dedicated machine instead of producing software to answer the needs made known to DECOY at the New Orleans NAR Convention.

Once the design of the *AdWriter* was completed, the next step was field testing. Machines were placed in "friendly" real estate firms in locations where DECOY also had real estate publications. Within a short time, almost every site reported a similar result: they liked the program, but could they please get rid of the machine. It turned out that the conclusion drawn from the lack of *NewsAd* sales was not valid–there was no significant computerphobia in the real estate offices. The agents who wrote the ads knew how to use computers and used them frequently. They were simply looking for software that would enable them to utilize their existing hardware investments.

The design team then spent 1988 rewriting *NewsAd* to deliver the software with more horsepower. More than two years had been wasted since *NewsAd* had been introduced at the NAR show in New Orleans. A new problem surfaced because many of the enhancements to *NewsAd* were aimed at real estate publishers–of which DECOY was one–not real estate agents. While the agents had asked for short ads, the new software merely truncated the full-blown versions of ads, ignoring the results of years of research on effective real estate advertising that DECOY had done. Enhancement after enhancement followed the same pattern: customers were given the semblance of what they asked for, but never the reality.

Why was the reality never given to the users? The fact that the Chairman was too intimately involved with day-to-day product design, and was "listening impaired" when it came to dealing with real estate agents in general made it difficult. He knew what made for a good classified advertisement and the agents were going to get that, willy-nilly. Table 2.1 presents a few of the comments presented by users (and former users) of the program over the years; there never was a list of responses to these comments beyond "No" or "They don't need that."

NewsAd 2 was deemed ready for the NAR Convention in San Francisco in November, 1988. Once again, as with the *AdWriter,*

TABLE 2.1. Customers' Needs versus Developer's Needs

Customer-perceived needs	Developer-perceived needs
Quick to use	Quick writing capability
Easy to enter data	Standardized data entry
Write short ads	Write "good" ads
Store data and ads	No storage needed
Send ads to newspaper	No communications allowed

DECOY chose to ignore the trend in the microcomputer industry and marketed *NewsAd 2* as a leased product with a five-dollar charge for each ad the software created. DECOY had tried this same fee basis with *CompuAd* several years before, with an resounding lack of success. Although the *NewsAd 2* software itself was well received on the show floor, the method of pricing was not. Booth personnel reported remarks such as "I don't lease anything" and complete dismay when prospects heard about the per-advertisement charge. Only one copy of *NewsAd 2* was "sold" at the show, versus 50 copies of *NewsAd*.

NewsAd 2 was clearly in trouble at this point. Although it was "objectively" superior in many ways to *NewsAd*, the market did not accept the pricing structure. The Chairman was finally convinced to license the program on a sliding scale depending upon the number of projected house listings for which the real estate firm would have to write ads. Although this was an improvement, there was so much resistance–or confusion–in the marketplace that sales never approached break-even. In November 1989, after a major sales effort at the Dallas, Texas, NAR Convention had still produced less-than-satisfactory results and national advertising and direct-mail campaigns had achieved almost nothing in the way of sales, marketing of both *NewsAd* and *NewsAd 2* was halted. DECOY had invested well over $1 million in the product and had little to show for it except inventory.

AutoAd was a product that closely paralleled *CompuAd*: it wrote classified advertisements for used cars. It used the same pattern of prioritizing the features of the item to create the advertisement. However, it was not a case of substituting "Tudor" car for "Tudor" house to produce an ad. Research conducted by DECOY showed that the buyer of a $5,000 car needed different information about the car than the buyer of a $50,000 car. Some exploratory work had been done on *AutoAd* as early as 1985; by 1987, a rudimentary user's manual had been created. The project received a large boost in 1988 when DECOY was asked to create a used-car advertising paper in a small Ohio city. DECOY personnel saw *AutoAd* as a natural adjunct to the nascent newspaper. Moreover, used car advertisements were the second-largest category of classified advertising in DECOY newspapers. Getting better performance for their advertisers out of this major category would enhance DECOY's image and give it an edge on competing newspapers.

After several months of negotiation and development, DECOY abandoned the idea of the newspaper. The company was left with an almost complete software product which seemed to fill a need in the used car industry. Mindful of the *CompuAd* experience detailed above, DECOY engaged National Market Measures (NMM), a market research firm, to hold focus groups to assess reactions from used car professionals to the concept of a computer program to write automobile advertisements. NMM was asked to find answers to three questions: How would used car professionals like to advertise? How do used car professionals currently write their advertisements? and How could *AutoAd* fit into either their current writing or how they would like to advertise?

NMM used telephone solicitation of used car professionals with a screening questionnaire which did not disguise the subject to be covered in the focus group. DECOY provided NMM a list of prospective members for the panel from current advertisers in two DECOY newspapers. The group was analyzed first by the moderator and other staff members at NMM based on notes and the tapes (NMM, 1989); the audiotapes were then reviewed by DECOY personnel.

Shortly after the focus group started, it was obvious that *AutoAd* would have limited appeal to used car professionals. One of *Auto-Ad*'s chief attractions was its ability to write an infinite variety of ads for a given car. One focus group participant said, "If I worked for 'X' Chevy and had fifty [identical] Chevy Cavaliers to write about, I might be interested." However, he felt that each of his vehicles was unique and therefore *AutoAd* would not solve any of his needs.

The focus group revealed the simplistic approach to ad writing used in the industry. The used car manager gets into the car and drives around the block. "By the time I've driven a hundred yards, I know what to say" in the ad. Thus, the used car professionals felt that their experience would lead them to write better ads than the computer, even though, by their own admission, they did not really *know* what to include in the ad, and the fact that they did not like to write the ads. The majority of advertisements used by members of the focus group were "two-liners" designed to reduce the cost of the ad, not raise its effectiveness. Designing effective ads seemed to be less of a concern to those in the group than was the cost of the ad. When the focus group members were allowed to use *AutoAd* to write sample ads, their pre-existing attitudes were strengthened. They could not see how the system would save them time. They did not like the idea of having to input all the data about the automobile–also a constant complaint about *CompuAd*–and they did not believe that the dealership would hire someone merely to input the data. In short, as presented to the focus group, *AutoAd* was unsalable.

The report from NMM was delivered in November 1989, to a corporate environment radically different from that which existed when the research was commissioned. *NewsAd 2* had failed in the marketplace and was no longer being marketed; there was pervasive gloom at DECOY headquarters about the future of any of DECOY's innovations. The results of the focus group were accepted as "probably representative" of used car professionals, that sales expectations for *AutoAd* would be problematical at best, and undoubtedly as expensive to attain as those for *NewsAd*. *AutoAd* was shelved.

Both *CompuAd/NewsAd* and *AutoAd* were technological successes and market failures. *CompuAd/NewsAd* creates ads vastly superior to those written by most real estate agents. The ads use richer language, make properties more attractive to buyers, and are written exactly to the size required by advertisers to match an advertising budget. The same claims could be made for *AutoAd*. Why did neither product make it in the marketplace? First, they both failed to answer any apparent need on the part of potential users. Second, *CompuAd* was flung into the marketplace in violation of all but two of Voss's success factors: the product champion was the Chairman, and planned innovation was corporate policy (and an appropriate policy given the market conditions at the time) at DECOY. Third, as the development process progressed from *CompuAd* to *NewsAd* to *AdWriter* to *NewsAd 2,* there was no concomitant systematic market research to see if the existing users had suggestions for improvements to the product, nor any rigorous research done at all. The randomly received comments from users, or those who had tried the programs and returned them because they did not fit their needs, were not considered as sources of information.

Table 2.1 presents only a few of the user comments made over the course of the years with the developer's response to them. In most cases the developer was reluctant to give customers what they wanted because he was afraid that he would lose control of the program, the output, and whatever competitive advantage he possessed as a publisher of real estate print media. The programs continued to be developer driven and to include only what the developer thought was important–mostly to his needs as a real estate publisher.

The major cause of failure for the entire *CompuAd* family of software was the fact that DECOY ignored the Marketing Concept. There was no inherent, product-caused source of the failure. A great deal of DECOY's resources (both money and time) would have been saved if the Marketing Concept had been followed. The Marketing Concept does not imply that all product ideas will succeed; far from it. However, by correctly applying the Marketing Concept, firms will uncover failure earlier in the development cycle, with much smaller losses.

Why did the Chairman adhere to the Marketing Concept in *Auto-Ad* and not with the *CompuAd* family? It would be gratifying to state that it was because I was involved at an early stage in the development of *AutoAd* which allowed me to guide the development process, and my absence until much later in *CompuAd's* development hindered such guidance. However, it is more probable that the Chairman had much less money and ego invested in *AutoAd* than he did in *CompuAd*, he allowed himself more flexibility in thought and action in that case. It is imperative, particularly in cases where new product development occurs in an entrepreneurial environment, to introduce the Marketing Concept into the product development process as early as possible. The *CompuAd* family example above shows what can happen when it is introduced too late; *AutoAd* shows what can happen when it is introduced early.

A recent computer trade journal editorial complained about the "bloated, over-designed software that we are faced with day after day," caused by "whizzy features" (Alsop, 1992). Features such as these tend to be neglected because of industry structure: reviewers are sophisticated users and focus on standard benchmarks. Too often, input from ordinary users is shunned because they "will not understand" the product or "dealing with them will be too demanding" of scarce resources which need to be applied to the next version of the product.

Users of a technology often have a larger stake in that technology than the developer. They frequently know what is wrong with or missing from the product before the developers have any inkling. The concept of "beta testing" in the software industry is a recognition of this fact. (See Herstatt and von Hippel, 1992, and Dolan and Matthews, 1993, for details about beta testing.) One observer reports that users frequently have led developers to produce new software (Voss, 1985a). Another actively encourages such a stance on the part of developers of all high-tech products, and with good reason (von Hippel, 1986); in a recent study more than 80 percent of respondents reported that their customers were their "best source for new product and service ideas" (*Marketing News,* 1992).

What are the chances for success of a product that requires a change in the work process? Unless a product clearly offers substantial benefits, users will not reorganize their methods of doing business. *AutoAd* was perceived as offering no such benefit. Fax machines, on the other hand, have been so perceived and have been bought in large numbers by all types and sizes of businesses. Further, the research to determine what users want *must* be done with the people who will actually use the new product.

Standards are often seen as a partial solution to this problem: if a product adheres to the standard interface, users will know what to expect. If a program adheres to standard data addresses, it will be less likely to affect a user's already complex array. But standards belong to the realm of the engineer and are dangerous things to marketers (Cahill, 1992). They focus attention on the product or service and away from where it belongs–the customer. This shift in focus can lead to price competition and razor-thin margins between parity products. Almost always, these products will end up being, as commodities, virtually interchangeable pieces.

I would like to add one more extended example of the perils of ignoring the Marketing Concept, this time in a pure service business–one without the taint of the least modicum of tangible, physical product which computer software may carry: the residential real estate business. Real estate agents have reputations among the general population somewhat above politicians but, perhaps, below used car salesmen and undertakers. Why? What is it about the person who sells one the most expensive item most people ever buy that leads so many people to form a negative image? Is it sins of commission? Sins of omission? Routines of stand-up comedians? Is it the methods of doing business that the agents practice? Is it the price they charge for their service (remembering that it is the seller who pays that charge)?

Yet another survey discussing the low esteem that some segments of the housebuying public have for real estate agents recently crossed my desk. This is not the first such survey to do so, nor will it be the last. Why do residential real estate agents have such a problem with their potential customers? Is there something that real estate management can do to alleviate this problem? A survey conducted by the Colorado Springs, Colorado, Board of Realtors on the image of realtors found that on most dimensions having to do with professionalism, the general public gave agents higher marks than the professionals expected to receive. Further, both the general public and sellers of houses rated agents higher than did house buyers. But fully 40 percent of the sellers said that the services performed by realtors were not worth the commission paid to them by the sellers (Brown, 1987). I would like to discuss some findings from a research project conducted by a client of mine and their implications for squeezing a service into a crowded market. (Some of the results of a portion of this research were reported in Cahill, 1994a.) There are probably fewer markets that are more crowded than residential real estate sales, for there are over 1,000,000 licensed agents in the United States.

DECOY, Inc., commissioned the American LIVES (Lifestyle, Interests, Values, Expectations, and Symbols) Division of Holen North America to conduct a survey of the real estate market of Denver, Colorado, to help in the creation of a new publication to serve the needs of the real estate market in that city with the possibility of taking the publication national as either a supplement to or replacement for its *Homes Illustrated* line (American LIVES, 1991). Because the publication would be innovative in the real estate publication industry, several kinds of questions never before systematically examined in real estate were probed. A survey instrument unique to this study was developed by American LIVES and DECOY; the mail survey instrument was 11 pages long. This survey process is unique because of the several areas it covered in one instrument: the house search process; features desired and their use in the house; and LIVES analysis of the house buyer.

The questionnaire asked several kinds of questions; taken together, the answers give a basis for analyzing several dimensions to the home purchase process. Among these are: why the respondents moved, type of house sought, preference for new versus pre-owned house, the house-search process, attitudes toward realtors and their services. Further, a typology of five categories of people in the local real estate market was developed for the purposes of allowing DECOY to segment its markets. There were 328 questionnaire items that were analyzed: 72 questions pertaining to values and 3 pertaining to demographics were utilized to produce the segmentation analysis; 63 items for analysis of parts of the market and the home search process, reduced by factor analysis and multidimensional scaling to 18 key dimensions; and 83 interior features and attitudes toward rooms of the house.

There was clear evidence from this survey that house buyers want more information about their choices in the market; many buyers now feel they are not receiving adequate information from realtors–or from other sources currently available, for that matter. The following survey responses support the thesis that there is a dearth of information available:

- I want to see ads that have both addresses and prices of houses–90 percent
- I want to see ads that have much more complete house descriptions–88 percent
- I want a publication that shows what the whole housing market looks like–76 percent
- I want a longer list of features in houses before I go look at them–75 percent

To further elaborate on these quantitative survey results, it is necessary to insert the results of two earlier qualitative studies on similar themes. National Market Measures was commissioned by DECOY in 1985 to perform a focus group primarily to determine how active participants in the real estate market used *Locus* in their shopping process (National Market Measures, 1985a). (This focus group will be reported in and more detail in Chapter 7.) "I want to see everything that's for sale . . . and the only way to do that is through a realtor, getting access to the [Multiple Listing] book," was one specific comment. Although this focus group consisted of only ten people and was conducted six years earlier than the American LIVES study, it is interesting that comments anticipating the model developed quantitatively surfaced in the focus group research.

National Market Measures did a series of focus groups in 1988 for *Locus* (the results of these focus groups will also be reported in much greater detail in Chapter 7); the groups were each formed of single VALS (a typology developed by SRI International and explained in Chapter 7) types–Belongers, Inner Directed, and Achievers (National Market Measures, 1988). Again, the primary purpose was not to determine the members' feelings about realtors. One series of questions concerned the reasons for changing residence and the process used for information search. In this set of focus groups, as in the previous group, there was general dissatisfaction expressed with the method needed to get a handle on the totality of the offerings for the metropolitan area. This was true even though most of the members of the focus groups were not moving into the Cleveland area but were long-term residents merely moving to another house, and who presumably would be at least somewhat knowledgeable about the market.

Given these extraordinarily high percentages of buyers who felt that they did not receive the information they wanted during a recent involvement in the housing market, it is clear that a tremendous amount of dissatisfaction exists in the way people have to look for houses. The problem is that standards required for good market information have risen, decade by decade, and realtors have not kept pace. This is hardly the view of realtors that the industry would like people to have. Nevertheless, it is confirmed by other research. Dunlap, Dotson, and Chambers (1988) surveyed both brokers and buyers and found that conflicting perceptions exist between the two as to the degree of customer orientation brokers exhibit. Houston and Sudman (1977) outline other dimensions of information which individuals wish to obtain from realtors–notably "quality of life" dimensions for a particular neighborhood–which were not being obtained. The upscale portion of the house-buying public has become acclimated to high-quality product information in almost any other market they participate in.

According to the results of the American LIVES survey, only 58 percent of the respondents made any use of a realtor to search for the house; an additional 16 percent made only what they considered "limited use" of one. Some other themes from this stage of the survey included that 87 percent wanted to use a realtor to gain access to various house listings; 85 percent wanted a realtor to help save time; and 85 percent mostly wanted a realtor to handle paperwork. Those who did not use a broker were more negative about them than those who did. Table 2.2 provides the findings based on the economic dimension of the American LIVES typology, as this dimension proved to be the item which sliced through the use of a realtor and the reasons for using one.

The implications of Table 2.2 are manifold. First, it would behoove realtors to pay attention to the house-buying process, even though, as agents of the seller, they are not working for the buyer. Realtors only get paid when the property sells; anything they can do to speed the process and increase their effectiveness in selling to buyers improves their productivity and efficiency as agents for the seller. Second, an entrepreneurial opportunity has been created for someone to provide a better information source for the search process; although some entrepreneurs have attempted to fill this void (see Cahill, 1990; Wiesendanger, 1991, and Chapter 8), it remains to be seen if the upscale buyers will pay for information which has traditionally been provided–however badly–for free. Third, there is a tremendous entrepreneurial opportunity present for a new type of real estate agent–the so-called buyer's agent, working for the buyer and not the seller–to develop the information and search tools. Although buyer's agents currently exist, they do not seem to have developed to the point of providing enough information to satisfy the needs of the upscale buyers. Levine (1983) discusses the con-

TABLE 2.2

SAMPLE

Median Search Time–3 months

58% enjoyed the time spent

19% used a newspaper

87% wanted a realtor mostly to gain access to listings

85% wanted a realtor to help save time

85% wanted a realtor mostly to handle the paperwork

62% said presearch information from realtor was very good to pretty good

"Upscale" Buyers

Drive through neighborhoods they are interested in

Have realtor drive them around to look at houses

Use Multiple Listing Books

Mostly want a realtor to handle paperwork

Would rather not have to use a realtor

Want a better listing service than currently available

"Downscale" Buyers

Search through newspapers, particularly suburban newspapers

Go to the realtor first

Find their house from an open house

Mostly want realtor to find the best loan

(But see Gersh (1989) and Newspaper Advertising Bureau (1986) for differing views of the importance of newspapers in finding a house. Also, see Gottko (1985), Gottko (1986), and McCarthy (1979) for importance of mobility in the process.)

cept of the buyer's broker and claims that it is an idea whose time has come.

The price of the services provided by a realtor are generally borne by the seller. Typically, that price is a percentage of the sales price, with all costs of selling the property–such as advertising–to be borne by the realtor. Although each metropolitan area has its own "customary" commission structure, percentages typically range from 5 percent to 7 percent of the sales price of the house; how this commission is split between the agent who obtained the listing and the agent who actually showed the house to the buyer is also subject to regional "custom." Change is starting to come to the industry, albeit slowly. There are firms–both national systems as well as locally owned firms–which will sell a house for a flat fee. Nonetheless, the percentage-of-sales-price fee is the norm. This system has caused very low productivity by agents–and buyers (Crockett, 1984). Further, by being fixed, brokerage costs are too high to the seller if a property sells quickly (Grigsby, 1984) and too low to the realtor if it must be heavily advertised. The fixed commission has encouraged firms to fight diversification and depend entirely on the "home run" approach of getting listings and selling them, instead of diversifying across a range of related real estate services as they have in Britain (Bordessa, 1979a). As such, pricing in the real estate industry is reminiscent of the securities brokerage business during its era of a fixed commission structure.

Starting with the pricing problem, restricting access to the Multiple Listing Service to members of local Boards of Realtors leads to antitrust problems (Trombetta, 1980). This restriction of information leads directly to people feeling "forced" to use a realtor to find out about listings, as mentioned in the American LIVES survey. In fact, unethical and unprofessional behavior are cited as potential problems with clients (Bordessa, 1979b; Edmonds and Lindbeck, 1987). In a recent survey sponsored by the National Association of Realtors, several attributes were displayed by agents of both satisfied buyers and sellers; the seven leading attributes were (Bleasdale, 1991):

- Keeps clients' best interests in mind
- Keeps clients up-to-date

- Knows the market
- Is professional
- Shows houses that are right for the buyer
- Knows financing programs
- Knows the neighborhood.

If this list looks familiar, it should; it approximates a definition of the Marketing Concept mentioned at the beginning of this chapter, at least as it would apply to the real estate industry. Is this a way out of the difficulties mentioned above which will only increase in the years to come for the real estate industry (Wallace, 1985)? I certainly think so.

So, where does all of this discussion of the Marketing Concept leave us? Obviously, I feel that the concept is valid, whether one is discussing high-tech products or low. Or services, even such antiquated and unchanging services as residential real estate brokerage. If one does not provide what one's customers want, one will not stay in business for very long. The Marketing Concept is a tool to use in developing new products and services. One needs to discover what customers want that is currently not available in the marketplace, as well as where what they want is being over-provided. The former is the method by which monopoly positions and new markets can be created, à la Federal Express. The latter is the way to simply provide another "me-too" offering–frequently at a lower price in order to attract any customers at all. This leads, not to "squeezing" another service into a crowded market, but rather "cramming" another service down the throat of an unwilling market–certainly a recipe for disaster if I ever heard of one.

I used to tell my marketing students, to paraphrase a line from Isaac Asimov's *Foundation* trilogy, that price competition was the last refuge of the incompetent. Any idiot can do it, although only the lowest cost producer can do it long term. There must be a technique, or set of techniques, which permits new service developers to find out what their prospects want that is currently not being provided in the market so that one can provide it. Chapter 3 will provide such a technique.

Chapter 3

Perceptual Mapping

What is perceptual mapping? In its marketing application, the term means a technique used to graphically represent the position of a particular offering in terms of all the other offerings in a specific category of products or services. There are generally two goals in mind when managers have perceptual maps drawn. The first is to determine where the offering is positioned with respect to the competitive offerings. The second is to help identify product or service attributes which are important to customers and which can be used to differentiate one's offering from the others in the category. No matter how important a particular attribute may be in the customer's mind, unless the customer perceives differences across offerings, that attribute will not be influential in customer's decisions when faced with choosing among alternatives. Frequently the attributes which customers find important are latent, and often unobservable (or, more usually, are deemed unimportant) by management; perceptual mapping helps in the essential task of uncovering these latent dimensions, and making them and their importance more apparent to all concerned.

Why do perceptual mapping? Very simply, because it is often easier for people to *see and understand* relationships when they are presented graphically rather than in columns of figures or in long verbal descriptions. The various techniques of perceptual mapping which will be presented below all deliver, as their final product, a graphic map of the various attributes, locating the different offerings already in the marketplace in space with relation to each other and with relation to the various attributes uncovered by quantitative surveying of customers and potential customers. The numbers used to create the maps can be presented to managers in tabular form, but they are not easy to interpret in that form. When they are presented to managers in the form of a graph or map, their interpretation is made easier; in fact the interpretation often becomes so obvious that decisions can be made very quickly and with little discussion.

From the process of perceptual mapping one hopes to derive the gaps in the current offerings in a market. Figure 3.1 shows a conjectural map of various orchestras and chamber-music groups in Cleveland, mapped along the dimensions of Amateur/Professional, and "Daringness of music programmed"–a measure of how much unfamiliar or new music that group presents. If one wanted to launch another group, some gaps in the current offerings are apparent. First, Apollo's Fire, recently established, jumps out from the Figure as filling a previous gap; it is a professional chamber group performing only Baroque music–there is nothing else in its niche. If I wanted to launch another professional group, I would look to the upper left quadrant–a small group playing very unusual music. I would not want to compete with the Cleveland Orchestra, nor with the Cleveland Chamber Symphony, which almost exclusively programs music of living composers. Are there other gaps?

Try Figure 3.2, a map on the Amateur/Professional dimension, but searching along another dimension–cost of tickets–which consumers would undoubtedly find important and which would give a new entrant a marketable differentiation. The Trinity Chamber Orchestra/Chamber Players perform primarily during a "brownbag" series of concerts, all of which are free and open to the public Wednesdays–and well attended–at noon in a near-downtown Episcopal Cathedral. In Figure 3.1, you can see that these concerts are not "daring," differentiating themselves from several similar small orchestras in the area only by being professional; many of the members of this group are members of the Akron Symphony or Canton Symphony–professional ensembles in smaller cities near Cleveland. Yet when the dimension of ticket price is used instead of "daringness," this group's uniqueness becomes quickly evident. As a frequent attendee at their concerts, I can also testify to the power of that free admission; when they charge even a nominal amount for a concert, attendence plummets. These maps would make it relatively easy for decision makers to start crafting a new group's offering so as not to compete head-on with other more established

FIGURE 3.1. Hypothetical Perceptual Map of Selected Cleveland Area Orchestras & Chamber Groups

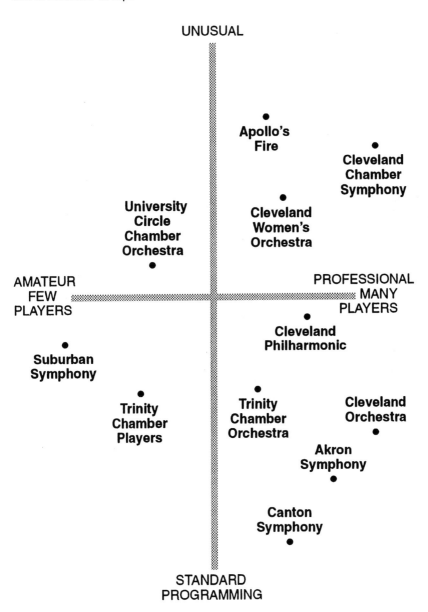

FIGURE 3.2. Hypothetical Perceptual Map of Selected Cleveland Area Orchestras & Chamber Groups

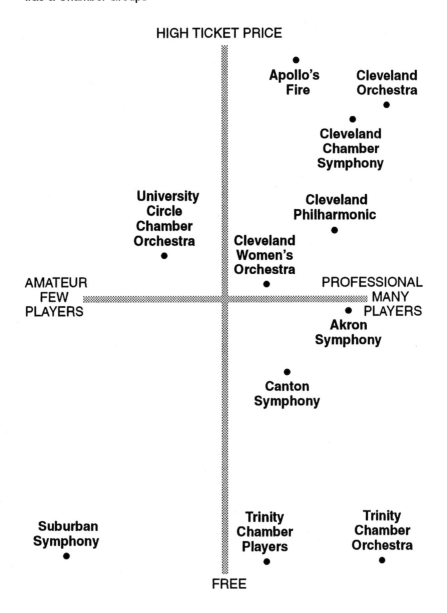

musical organizations in town; "me-tooism" works no better in cultural offerings than in soap.

There have not been many examples in the published literature of perceptual maps for services. One of the few was presented in Horne, McDonald, and Williams (1986). The authors randomly contacted an entire area code for respondents to evaluate 43 services on 25 different dimensions, ranging from tangibility of effects, personnel versus equipment performing the service, social risk, and financial risk, to amount of face-to-face contact. A rather complete map was prepared based upon the results. Sisodia (1993) did a study of how brokerage firms and financial institutions select one another. Two multidimensional scaling techniques were used to develop perceptual maps of clusters of firms selling clusters of attributes.

So much for the explanation of why should one do perceptual mapping. How does one go about doing the job? There are three basic techniques which I will discuss in the next section: factor analysis, discriminant analysis, and multidimensional scaling. Each has its uses–and advocates. Kohli and Leuthesser (1993) in a recent article aimed directly at managers, outlined these three techniques and compared their strengths and weaknesses, and described when to use which. Much of the following section is based on their article combined with other material–and all made as applications-oriented and nonacademic as possible. Nevertheless, I strongly recommend that the actual design of the surveys and preparation of the perceptual maps themselves be done by researchers who are trained in the techniques, although software designed to aid in these techniques is becoming more accessible all the time.

TECHNIQUES

Factor Analysis is essentially a data-reduction technique in which the objective is to represent the original assembly of a large number of attributes in terms of a (one hopes much) smaller number of underlying dimensions or factors. After the factors have been identified, the brands' ratings on these factors are used to position the brands in perceptual space. The first step is to produce "Factor Loadings," which is roughly analogous to a set of correlation statistics. Each factor loading is a measure of the importance of the variable in measuring each factor. The "explanation of variance" in the variable is displayed numerically in the Factor-Loading Table as a single statistic–analogous to the R^2 in multiple regressions. After all of this statistical work is completed, it is possible to take the data points and plot them into a graph, thus showing graphically where each of the offerings lies–a powerful tool.

Cluster Analysis may be used to identify offerings that are similar along some criteria. As a technique, it is less sophisticated than factor analysis, but it is also easier to perform. The purpose of cluster analysis is to group offerings into a small number of mutually exclusive groups with quite similar characteristics so that they may be discussed as if they were a single offering. It is a technique that is frequently employed in doing market-segmentation studies. A glance at Figure 3.3 will show that the current newspaper offerings in Cleveland fall into clusters (Figure 3.3 is hypothetical). Cluster analysis should also be prepared based upon quantitative surveys of actual customers.

Discriminant Analysis is also used to reduce the number of attributes to a smaller number of underlying dimensions. However, discriminant analysis focuses on the attributes which show differences between offerings. Discriminant analysis tends to ignore attribute ratings which show large variations within offerings and focuses instead on attribute ratings which show large variations between offerings (or, to put it another way, from one respondent to another). A major difference in the method of presentation is that in the perceptual maps prepared from discriminant analysis, it is possible to assess how strong the agreement among respondents on one factor is in relation to other factors.

In their comparison of factor analysis and discriminant analysis, Kohli and Leuthesser (1993:18) give a roadmap of when to use discriminant and when to use factor analysis. Discriminant analysis should be preferred when there are objective dimensions to measure. The two techniques can be used complementarily to highlight substantial differences in agreement among consumers. And factor analysis should be preferred when there are few offerings in a category. Given these conditions, coupled with those of service categories generally–and professional service in particular–most of

FIGURE 3.3. Hypothetical Perceptual Map of Selected Cleveland Newspapers

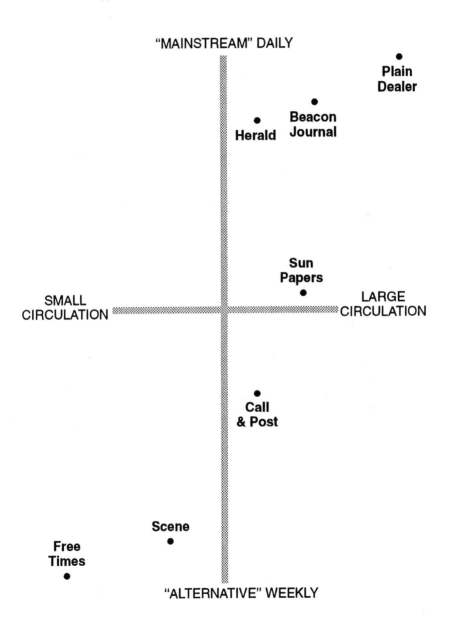

the time factor analysis will be preferred over discriminant analysis, if for no other reason than service offerings have so few objectively determinable dimensions, and there are often few offerings in a category, particularly when one runs a cluster analysis on the offerings. Although there may be literally dozens of law firms operating in a city, for example, by the time the potential clients have reviewed the list, there may be only two or three clusters, each containing dozens of firms which look substantially alike to the client.

Multidimensional Scaling (MDS) maps the offerings spatially, so that their relative position in the mapped space reflects the degree of perceived similarity between them. Respondents evaluate–either in rank-order or rate–the offerings in pairs, judging the overall similarity between the paired offerings. Unlike either factor analysis or discriminant analysis, MDS asks respondents to rate offerings on overall similarity, not individual attributes.

Kohli and Leuthesser (1993:15-16) suggest some considerations in making the decision whether to use MDS, factor analysis or discriminant analysis. First, MDS works better the larger the number of offerings available for respondents; in markets where there are only a few offerings (such as the Cleveland newspaper market), MDS loses power. Offsetting this desirability of large numbers of offerings is the fact that the larger the number of offerings, the more complex the rating or rank-ordering job that faces respondents, calling into question some of the real-world validity of the results. Third, MDS requires only similarity judgments for the pairings; therefore, it is not necessary to do prior research to determine which product or service attributes are important in consumer choice. Thus, when it is not clear that the relevant attributes can be specified for respondents, Kohli and Leuthesser recommend using MDS.

In discussions with several market researchers about why these techniques are not used more frequently, two major points were developed. First, as I reviewed the literature on perceptual mapping I noticed that much of the academic work was done in the late 1970s and early 1980s (see L. Cooper, 1983, for a review), and that relatively little has been done more recently–although these techniques still appear in marketing research textbooks. Since there has been relatively little recent academic interest, it stands to reason that the techniques have not been taught much. Cooper's paper cited

158 academic articles, papers, book chapters, and books relating only to MDS and its impact on marketing subjects spanning the field, including product planning, market structure analysis, market segmentation, pricing, branding, channels of distribution, personal selling, and advertising – but the article is now a decade old.

There is one recent article that offers some exciting applications of what a practitioner would call "quick and dirty" mapping. Steven Shugan (1987) estimated brand positions by regression of aggregate sales data based upon output from supermarket scanners. He concluded that managers can derive a perceptual map, albeit not a map with a great deal of richness of raw information, from observed choice behavior as delivered by supermarket scanners in such abundance. Managers can then study the direct effect of both a brand's price and its positioning on sales. Unfortunately, "pure" services cannot be handled in such a manner, although the product portion of a service–such as McDonald's hamburgers or Domino's pizza–certainly could be. Nevertheless, Shugan's article is interesting as it continues to use an old technique.

Second, there seem to be a few research firms which use these techniques as rather standard tools in their kit, but most firms do not use them at all. The firms which do use the techniques tend to use them a lot. The Marketing Decisions Group at Wyse Advertising in Cleveland has long been an avid practitioner of perceptual mapping, primarily MDS. Their favorite computer program for analysis is MDPREF, since it is an internal form of analysis where only the original data are used in interpretation, whereas in some other techniques additional information is employed (Kowalysko, n.d., a and b). Although there are arguments for one program over another, they are not important here. What is important is that the tools are readily available and understood by most marketing PhDs, so finding a researcher to produce and interpret the perceptual maps should not be a problem in most communities in the United States.

Whose perceptual maps should be used? The easy and obvious answer is the potential customers'. But this is only part of the answer. The offering firm's employees also have impressions of the new offerings that are important to take into consideration, particularly if it is a service offering that is under discussion. Stell and Fisk (1986) discuss the use of images and their creation in services in some detail. The service offered needs to be closely aligned with the service demanded, or there will be many problems for the firm. In short, both customers' and employees' perceptual maps need to be drawn and taken into consideration when designing and implementing the new offering. To the fullest extent possible, the two sets of maps need to be made congruent before launch; however, the management needs to be totally aware of any lack of congruence and needs to work toward making them congruent. But that is a different story and a different book–one about internal marketing.

Why are these techniques not used more in new product and new service introductions? The most important impediment seems to be the fact that the research necessary to produce perceptual maps must be done no later than the design of the product or service for it to do the most good. And this is just the time when firms are the most distracted.

Ideally, the stages of new service introduction should flow from idea to decisions about how practicable the introduction of this new service will be to design. During the decision stage, some sort of perceptual mapping of the existing offerings should be performed, allowing the firm to discover gaps in the services offerings the competition makes so that the new service can be designed to fill those gaps, and thus be made more attractive to potential customers. Whether a firm is a start up or an existing firm trying to expand its offerings, this does not seem to be the time when anyone wants to do basic consumer research. Service design (as well as product design) seems to run more from a firm's internal capabilities rather than what the market wants or where there are gaps that certain customers are looking for. And, predictably, so many of the new offerings fail after introduction.

Why this reluctance to embrace (or, perhaps, re-embrace) a technique which I feel would be so beneficial in designing and introducing new services? One reason it is the cost involved, for it does require some amount of marketing research; a survey of some sort must be designed and administered to customers or potential customers. But, I suspect, that more important than the cost is the fact that research at this point in the new product/new service process is perceived by too many people as something that slows down the process, that would prevent the new service from being introduced in a timely manner. However, as shown in the *NewsAd/AutoAd* comparison in Chapter 2, sometimes slowing down the process is exactly what the firm needs to do, to allow more time to reflect upon what it is about to offer to the public. Also, as mentioned above, the new service process too often proceeds on the basis of what the firm can offer rather than what the public wants; perceptual mapping techniques can throw into high relief very quickly–and painfully to its champion–whether the firm is about to embark upon this type of new service introduction.

Am I claiming too much for perceptual maps? After all, if they are so good and powerful and easy to produce and interpret, why do so few firms use them? This is a valid question. In the three cases which follow, I do not claim that producing perceptual maps would have made any of these new services a success; far from it. Nevertheless, I would say that developing perceptual maps prior to the introduction of the services would have (possibly) stopped the publisher from introducing one or possibly two of them; the third could have been better designed to fit the market demand. Stopping the introduction of services which will have difficulty succeeding is, as I mentioned in Chapter 2, a valid goal and one for which we should strive. I believe that perceptual maps are tools which can work in that direction.

PART II.
CASE EXAMPLES

Chapter 4

Why Media Cases?

The three case studies which follow trace the conception, development, introduction into the market, and ultimate demise of three services: two newspapers aimed at specific, small slices of readership in a larger market and an interactive computer system aimed at buyers of residential real estate. I was personally involved in two of these ventures as a consultant/employee; the third I was involved with in several guises.

In addition to cited material from the reference list at the end of this book, I have made extensive use of personal recollections, and recorded and unrecorded conversations and interviews with dozens of participants in all three cases. Although the use of these recollections violates some strict academic conventions, I have included them for three reasons. First, I cannot think of these cases without these recollections because I was so intimately involved with them. Second, I believe that without including this material, the case presentations would be critically weakened–unnecessarily, as this book is not aimed at an academic audience. Please be reassured that I have made no major alteration of fact (so far as I remember it) to make my points clearer; at most I have changed a name or two to protect an individual's privacy. Third, I am a firm believer in the validity of what is called "Qualitative Research," one strand of which–Participative Inquiry or Participant Observation–fits with the method I used to build these cases (Reason, 1994; Clandinin and Connelly, 1994). Simply stated, I have become a valid source of data for explanation because I was a participant in much of what I am describing. Qualitative research as a series of methods is beginning to build a following in many academic disciplines, including many of the business areas–although it is not universally accepted.

Given these three cases, qualitative research is the only way to present them.

Why these three cases? First of all because I *was* so intimately involved: I know these operations. Second, and much more important, they are all media operations: two were newspapers and the third was an interactive advertising medium designed in part to supplement and in part to replace a newsprint magazine medium.

All three of the following cases involve a service that was free to consumers; getting people to pick up the papers was not difficult at all, nor was it difficult to induce people to try InfoVision. Consumers had no financial risk in using the service. Like all free media, these three examples were financially supported by advertisers–and the entrepreneur. The advertisers did have financial (and reputation) risk involved in using these new media: would readers/users respond? Would anyone know? How?

Advertisers are willing to spend advertising dollars on a particular medium only to the extent that they perceive they are getting value from those dollars; they perceive that their target market uses the medium; customers and prospects tell them that they have seen or heard the advertisement; or they see customers in their establishment with the medium in hand (impossible, of course, for an electronic medium). Thus it is essential for media owners to convince two disparate and often antagonistic markets that it is in their best interests to use the medium: advertisers have to be shown meaningful readership or viewership numbers; readers and viewers have to be shown good editorial content. It is difficult to determine which is the chicken and which is the egg; one of the following cases had its readers before its advertiser, one had its advertisers before its readers, and one never got any real advertisers. In the case of a free-to-readers publication, editorial content frequently has to walk an additional fine line between being cooperative with the advertisers (who, after all, are paying for the medium and do not want to see negative stories–and frequently think anything less-than-positive is negative–about them in the paper) while at the same time not seeming to let them control the publication, or readers may quit reading the publication. The Cleveland *Edition* had severe problems in this regard. This Janus-faced stance of media makes for a special relationship to several markets, and they are thus very distinctive and very sensitive to problems with those markets.

Therefore, I have chosen the three cases which follow because they bring into high relief some of the problems inherent in introducing a new service into a market, whether the firm is a non-profit entity or not. A former colleague and I have often discussed this model of a Janus-faced market, where enterprises have to serve two (or more) often diametrically opposed segments, as a paradigm for nonprofit organizations. They have at least two radically different "markets" to satisfy: the users of the service, and those who contribute to the organization, supplying the funds for the users. Often these two groups have virtually nothing in common, never have contact with each other, and probably would not like each other if they met. Nevertheless, the organization has to serve both segments well, or it cannot fulfill its function of serving its users. The organization cannot afford to affront either segment, for without both wheels, it ceases to be viable.

THE PERILS OF A "ONE-NEWSPAPER TOWN"

In June 1982, the Cleveland *Press*–an afternoon daily newspaper–ceased publication. Henceforth, Cleveland would be condemned to be that anathema to big-city dreams of selfhood–the "one-newspaper town." Although the *Plain Dealer* continued in operation as the seven-mornings-a-week newspaper, and gleefully advertised itself as the "largest newspaper in Ohio," it remained unloved, particularly by the media community in Cleveland. Its role in the demise of the *Press* has remained shadowy and filled with some of the same conspiracy messages that surround the assassination of President Kennedy.

Nevertheless, Cleveland was never truly a one-newspaper town. Within a week of the death of the *Press* there were several daily newspapers being sold on the streets of Cleveland from newspaper boxes: the Akron *Beacon-Journal,* from that city less than an hour to the southeast; the Lorain *Journal,* from that city less than an hour to the west; and the Lake County *News-Herald,* from the suburbs directly to the east. Two major chains saturated the Cuyahoga County suburbs with weekly newspapers on Thursday. Additional-

ly, there was a large weekly newspaper serving the black community, a very successful and journalistically first-class paper serving the
large Jewish community, and a newspaper published by the Catholic diocese. And, extremely important to the discussion of the
Cleveland *Edition* below, there was a long-time entertainment
weekly–the *Scene*–which primarily catered to rock music fans and
the establishments which featured rock. This list, while not totally
inclusive–for instance, it does not include any of the foreign-lan-
guage papers which still survived in Cleveland's ethnic communities in the early 1980s–belies the description of Cleveland as a
"one-newspaper town." What most of the users of that phrase
seemed to mean is that no other "major" daily was published in
Cleveland; all the other dailies were published in what Clevelanders
have always regarded as second-tier cities (at best), and thus not of
the same quality as the *Press*.

Throughout much of its last years the *Press* was seen more as a
nonentity than the "great paper" it became after its death. In fact, it
had bought the other afternoon newspaper–the *News*–in the late
1950s and suffered obloquy for so doing, as the *News* had been a
"great newspaper." But by the early 1980s the day of the afternoon
newspaper was over. The *Press's* circulation was in a death spiral,
leading to a decline in advertising revenue, which led to a decline in
dollars for editorial, which led to a decline in readers. . . . In
desperation, the *Press* tried a Sunday edition, tried editorial color,
tried big promotions, tried anything that they could think of to keep
going. Everything failed.

However, there was a degree of angst that was palpable for
weeks after the *Press* died as writers and others figuratively wan-
dered the streets of Cleveland bemoaning the loss of a paper "superior" to the *Plain Dealer*. Of course it is difficult to conceive that
the paper was so superior to the *Plain Dealer* if it failed in the
marketplace, but writers operate under different rules from marketers and bemoaned the loss of this allegedly superior product. It was
this angst more than anything else which led to the establishment of
the Cleveland *Edition,* the subject of Chapter 5.

More than the writers–and the few readers the *Press* had left
when it folded–the major advertisers in Cleveland bemoaned the
loss of the *Press,* even if they did not advertise in it. Within a few

months, advertising rates at the *Plain Dealer* rose as that paper began flexing its muscles in what was perceived to be a monopoly situation. Although many advertisers felt the pinch of the new rates, few were in a position to do anything about it but complain. However, two groups of advertisers were in a position and one of them–the large real estate firms–did something about it. That decision is the subject of Chapter 7. The other group–car dealers–also attempted to do something to break the *Plain Dealer*'s monopoly. After some time of paying the higher rates, representatives of the Greater Cleveland Automobile Dealer's Association contacted both chains of suburban weekly newspapers mentioned above, with the idea of inducing one of them to put out an automobile advertising section. The Sun chain published *Sun Wheels* for a short time, apparently without much success.

The feelings of large advertisers against "one-newspaper towns" can surface long after a second paper has closed down, or even if there were never two dailies in a community. DECOY Inc., was contacted by the auto dealers association of another Ohio city to establish a stand-alone automobile weekly tabloid newspaper, modeled loosely on what the real estate community was getting with *Locus*. Although for several reasons DECOY never published this newspaper, the weak position into which large advertisers feel that they are trapped in "one-newspaper towns" when it comes to negotiating advertising rates in those papers, and the need to be in that paper because "everyone gets it," or "everyone else advertises there" is a major factor in *business* decisions to start some sort of paper to compete with the daily, even if it is only for that particular niche, like *Locus* or the car papers mentioned above. The impact of this perception will be discussed in Chapter 7.

Chapter 5

The Life and Death and Life and Death and Life and Death of the Cleveland *Edition*– An Alternative Newspaper

When the Cleveland *Press* suspended publication in June 1982, Bill Gunlocke, a graduate of Notre Dame University and a former English teacher in the Cleveland school system, was managing a bookstore in downtown Cleveland. On August 5, 1984, 40,000 copies of his new alternative newspaper, the Cleveland *Edition,* were on the streets. A small folded tabloid paper distributed free of charge, the *Edition* was almost excruciatingly hip and anti-establishment and carried extensive negative coverage of the *Plain Dealer,* Cleveland's remaining daily newspaper. The design was good, the writing adequate and feature-oriented, but the advertising was almost nonexistent. The *Edition* suspended publication in May of 1985 for lack of money, but with a promise to its readers that it would be back when Gunlocke was able to raise more money.

The paper came back in October 1987, with a slightly different look, although the basic design hammered out in 1984 remained. This time, the back page was sold to Higbee's, Cleveland's largest department store. Having the back page sold, and to such a mainstream advertiser, held the promise of more revenue stability; also, having the largest department store aboard held the promise that other advertisers, with their herd mentality when it comes to trying new media, might sign on this time. But after Roldo Bartimole–one of the writers who will reappear in this story–wrote a piece stating that the erection of the Galleria (a very upscale mall downtown) might make it difficult for the two remaining downtown department stores to continue to succeed, Higbee's cancelled their back page advertisement. The *Edition* apparently weathered this storm, but was eventually forced to suspend publication once more in April 1989, again with a promise from Gunlocke that he would be back after he had raised more money.

Gunlocke found the money, and the *Edition* resumed publication in October 1989. By this time the stable of writers included such people as Roldo Bartimole, a former *Wall Street Journal* reporter and publisher of *Point of View,* a vitriolic anti-establishment newsletter devoted especially to skewering everyone connected with United Way; Mary Grimm, now an instructor of creative writing at Case Western Reserve University, published novelist, and a writer whose short stories have appeared in the *New Yorker*; Mark Winegardner, an instructor of creative writing at John Carroll University, with more than one published book about sports and sports figures to his credit; and Doug Clarke, former *Press* sports writer and well respected in Cleveland. There were other good writers who came and went, and some who would contribute only one piece and never be seen again. The writing level had vastly improved. But the level of advertising was still quite low.

By April 1992, the paper was clearly in trouble–again. There had been negotiations with additional (unnamed) investors which ultimately broke down; although these negotiations had been conducted secretly, "everyone" knew about them. On April 30, 1992, the *Edition* hit the streets with a picture of Gunlocke standing behind one of his (empty) boxes with a placard saying only "Help!" In an editorial entitled "An Immodest Proposal," Gunlocke appealed to his still-large readership for money in several guises: donations, subscriptions for what would continue to be a free paper, or the chance to become a shareholder. This appeal failed, and the paper suspended publication for the last time shortly thereafter. On September 30, 1992, the paper that has sometimes been sarcastically called "Son of the *Edition*"–the *Free Times*–began publication.

The *Free Times*'s original publisher, Richard Siegal, was one of the individuals who had entered negotiations with Gunlocke to invest in the *Edition.* The initial editorial staff of the *Free Times* was almost totally composed of alumni of the *Edition:* Bartimole, Winegardner, Eric Broder, and Ken Myers, who had edited the *Edition,* along with several others. Further, the production manager had come along. As of today, the *Free Times* continues to survive, despite the departure of its founding editor–to pursue his freelance writing career–and the death of Richard Siegal a year after the paper's inception. But the *Free Times* is not the only "Son of the *Edition*"; *City Reports*–now defunct–was started by Gunlocke's former partner Tom Reidy, brought in to the *Edition* to provide business leadership, and *The River Burns,* also now defunct but replaced by *The Tab*–a large, tabloid monthly–was started by Rick Ferrell, former advertising manager at the *Edition.* So in this one sense of reproducing young, the *Edition* successfully lives on. This is no small accomplishment.

But without a doubt, the *Edition* was business failure. Not once, not twice, but three times. And the question must be asked: Why? Why did this paper fail? It printed between 30,000 and 40,000 copies per week, and people picked them up; it was *read* and talked about; it has spawned a seemingly prosperous successor with a stable of authors who got their start and much of their early local exposure in its pages. How could a paper with that kind of readership fail?

Two answers arise almost immediately, but I think they need to be rejected. First is the obvious "undercapitalized entrepreneurial venture." Although the *Edition* may have been undercapitalized, it published for almost five years, spread over the almost eight calendar years of its existence; if lack of capital had been a severe problem, the paper would never have lasted so long. Gunlocke spent large amounts of his and other peoples' money during the life of the *Edition*. Although the exact figure is immaterial–and I do not know that anyone knows it exactly, what with some investments having been made in kind (such as the office rent) and others having been made in cash–the net loss on the paper totalled somewhere in the mid-six-figure range. For the "undercapitalized entrepreneur" hypothesis to hold a significant amount of accuracy, there must be some degree of certainty that if the *Edition* had had a million dollars to spend (or some other number), it would have succeeded. I doubt it. Second is the theory, propounded by one of my clients, that the real problem with the *Edition* was that it was not started in the mid-1970s as were most of the other alternative papers in the country. And that by the time the *Edition* came along, its "natural" market was not interested in that kind of a paper. There is some truth in this hypothesis.

The *City Paper* of Baltimore had 200 tabloid pages in its September 13, 1991, edition which was in Volume 15; at the same time, the *Edition* was struggling to publish 24 pages. In a memo to my client about alternative newspapers and the wisdom of his investing in the *Edition,* I made some propositions that I believe are relevant to the discussion of the causes of the *Edition*'s failure. First, readers of alternative papers seem to fall into two broad categories: leading-edge baby boomers (those born between 1945-1962)–the generation that was of college age during the Vietnam War–and (according to the VALS typology) the Inner Directed. During the life of the *Edition,* these groups were at the beginning of their traditional peak earning years, family formation years, houseowning years, etc. Yet this generation, of which I am a member, has not become their parents. They live in the suburbs, but are not "suburban." This generation's heroes are prematurely dead: the Kennedy brothers, Martin Luther King Jr., John Lennon. . . . The best of the alternative press addresses its readers in Big Picture terms; the worst simply treats its readers to anger and stale issues.

The *Edition*'s writers frequently expressed anger–but usually over local issues and almost never over national issues; the writers were locally based, so this makes sense. Here is one point where the *Free Times* differs from the *Edition*: the former is willing to take stories of national impact from other alternative papers. Had the *Edition* been started earlier, it probably would have developed some momentum to carry it along as its baby boom readers aged and their issues of choice and focal points changed. Since it did not start then, it seemed to miss. Gunlocke's answer to what he wanted to accomplish with the *Edition* in a *post mortem* interview is telling in this regard: "The idea of a campus paper comes to mind, a college paper for people who weren't in college any more. . . . [Open] and candid and searching like students are, and creative and bright" (Johnston, 1992:6). This probably could serve as the goal for most of the alternative papers of the last 25 years.

If neither undercapitalization nor starting too late was the cause for the *Edition*'s downfall, what was? A major part of the answer can also been seen in another *post mortem* interview with Gunlocke (Zoslov, 1992).

Were you in it to make money at all?

No, but I thought I would. I thought it would be impossible not to make money at this. I looked at the papers around the country and they seemed full of ads. We have many of the same type store here, why don't we get those? After a while, without the entertainment money coming in, I realized that, because of our opinionated columnists, we had become like *The New Republic* or *The Nation,* both of which I think are great, but both of which have never made any money. I guess it would have been a dream to win a foundation prize and be able to grubstake ourselves forever, without having to worry about the bottom line.

You didn't want to play the game?

I guess. Hard to believe that is the game, but apparently that is the game. I'm not good at schmoozing. I don't know if I'm above it. It's just not in me to accentuate somebody's concert or overenthuse about some new club that's opening. I created a vehicle with good writers thinking that those places would advertise in the paper and that they would overenthuse all they wanted to in their ads.

So, you're not the business type?

Obviously. I knew you had to put salespeople on the street. But I'm just not drawn to the commerce of things. I was in the book business; I'm a schoolteacher. I'm not a shopper, racing around to stores, trying to convince them to buy. I'm sure that attitude of mine, voiced or not, probably was felt. I never blew a horn or rang a bell when we sold an ad. (Johnston, 1992:6)

How could someone who dreamed of winning a prize so that he would not have to soil his hands with commerce, who thought that firms would "just advertise," find himself in a position to run through more than half-a-million dollars and wreck his enterprise in the process? This is a good question, but one that is unanswerable in our free enterprise system beyond a restatement of the bigger-fool hypothesis. Nevertheless, part of an answer appears in a story in *The River Burns,* allegedly tracing how that publication came into being.

> [Jim Deetz, cofounder] What we got to do is come up with a business run by people who aren't that bright or that talented. An industry totally staffed by nincompoops, wannabes and bedwetters. Come on, Rick, think: What business do you know, and know very well, where every single individual we've both encountered, especially in management, are complete and total bucketheads.
>
> [Rick Ferrell, cofounder] Publishing? . . . Publishing! . . . You're right. That's a business even you and I could do well in. (Dietz and May, 1993:7)

And remember that Ferrell had worked at the *Edition*; Deetz had worked at *City Reports.* Neither of these endeavors seems to have been a paragon of management expertise. But, at least in the case of the *Edition,* bad "management" does not seem to be the problem; the paper got out on time every week, with no blank spots where stories arrived too late to be included or advertising copy came in too late. Until funds ran drastically low, bills were paid–albeit late– and accounts receivable were collected, albeit not efficiently.

What went wrong with the *Edition?* Simply put, Gunlocke and his string of advertising managers (five of them during the paper's seven-year existence) were unable to turn a focused and relatively large readership into a coherent market that advertisers would buy. Remember my comment earlier that media outlets have two markets to serve simultaneously. The *Edition* successfully developed–and developed rather quickly–a loyal and devoted readership, a readership that looked for the paper every week, a readership that read the paper every week, a readership that looked forward not once but twice to the return of the *Edition* from publication suspensions.

But the potential advertisers stayed away in droves. A brief comparison between the *City Paper* of Baltimore of September 13,

1991, with the *Edition* of October 24, 1991 (the paper in my posses-
sion closest to the *City Paper*'s date), is useful and instructive in this
regard. The *City Paper*'s pages two through five are full-page ads for:
a restaurant delivery service, Marlboro cigarettes (Gunlocke, a smoker
himself, refused to run tobacco ads in his paper on moral grounds), a
men's clothing store, and an attorney. The *City Paper* contains 26 other
full-page ads, as well as three two-page spreads. Although some of
these large ads were the "usual" alternative-press mix of futons,
"head-shops," restaurants, and entertainment, some were mainstream
advertisers such as Toys R Us, and co-op advertising for automobile
parts and supplies; further, one of the two-page spreads was for "tour-
ist" attractions in southern Pennsylvania. In all, over one-half of the
paper's first 173 pages were display advertising of one sort or another;
the last 25 pages were classified and display classified advertisements,
largely help wanted and real estate–both rental and for sale. In contrast,
the *Edition* had only three full-page ads in its 36 pages (one of its
all-time biggest issues); one of those was traded-out for rent in its
office building, one was classifieds, and two pages were "personals."
It contained only one column of real estate-for-rent ads, no real estate-
for-sale, and seven help wanted ads. No "mainstream" advertisers
were included at all.

Why the difference between the papers? Part of the difference
has been alluded to above: the *City Paper* started much earlier and
has built an advertising following; the *Edition* had too many advertising managers, and Gunlocke had an "attitude." Nevertheless,
these cannot explain the whole disparity.

In 1986, prior to restarting the paper the first time, Gunlocke
developed a business plan in conjunction with one of the major
accounting firms in Cleveland. As part of that business plan, management commissioned a study through Case Western Reserve University in an effort to gauge the interest in the *Edition* of the advertising community (Drollinger, 1986). As part of the study, 18
individuals in 14 advertising agencies were surveyed by telephone,
as well as 44 representatives of 42 past or potential advertisers.
Although the telephoner was professionally qualified and the survey instrument reasonably well designed (it allowed great freedom
of answers to well-defined questions), the concept behind the survey is troubling, for reasons I will discuss later.

In response, advertising agency representatives answered a firm "yes" when asked, "Does Cleveland need such a paper." However, when asked if the *Edition* was appropriate for their clients, only half of the agencies said "yes" or "maybe." Does this dichotomy perhaps reflect the representatives answering "yes" as readers, and "no" or "maybe" as businesspeople? I think so. My suspicion is made firmer since the most common response to the question, "What would make the *Edition* a viable advertising vehicle for you (to use for clients)?" was, "A verified circulation audit." This problem recurs in the discussions of *Locus* in Chapter 7; there is a prejudice against free publications in the advertising community because they cannot quote accurate circulation figures to their clients when they ask, "How many people am I buying?" This problem also occurs in controlled circulation trade journals, although business-to-business advertisers are not so hesitant about advertising there because others do it and have for years, frequently with very good results. But in consumer advertising, there is no past history of using free distribution.

When faced with such a demand–understandable on the part of the advertising community–what should *Edition*'s management have done? An audit of a free circulation newspaper would not have a great deal of validity. But a readership survey should have been one of the first items on management's agenda. Management got around to commissioning a reader survey late in 1990, but the results–although reported in the newspaper editorially as soon as they were available–never made it into a media kit. In fact, the *Edition* never really had a media kit. When potential advertisers called in for information, they usually were just given rate information.

The survey of advertisers and potential advertisers was even more emphatic than that of advertising agencies about Cleveland's need for a paper like the *Edition*–perhaps reflecting advertiser's concern about monopoly power of the *Plain Dealer*. Several people contacted spoke of Cleveland's status as a one-newspaper town, and that the *Edition* would fill a void between the *Plain Dealer* and the *Scene* (this was particularly true for restaurant and entertainment advertisers). Several respondents mentioned the importance of regular calls by salespeople for their happiness with the paper.

As a final part of the survey, editors and publishers from 11 alternative weeklies from around the country were also contacted to find out how they did things. When asked "What did you have to do to convince advertisers that your paper was worthwhile?" four themes were dominant.

First, the single most important aspect was demand by readers and the resulting response to advertisements. As mentioned earlier, advertisers will not spend money on a medium that does not generate directly perceived responses. It does not have to be in the form of sales, but advertisers must at least know that their customers see or hear their advertisements. This is the reason for the age-old tag of "Tell our advertisers that you saw their ad in. . . ."

The second response was the need for market research to describe clearly who the paper's audience is, and what the paper's penetration of the desired segment(s) is in numbers that are meaningful to advertisers. Although this response is countervailing to some of the concern of advertising agencies–the desire on the part of agencies for big numbers covering the entire marketplace rather than smaller numbers on a specific segment (another problem that will surface again in Chapter 8)–this objection to segment/niche versus total market coverage can be dealt with. The suburban newspapers have been doing so successfully for decades.

The third response was dependability–distributing the paper consistently in the same place at the same time each week until picking up the paper becomes a habit for readers. This was never a problem with the *Edition*.

The fourth response was that management had to hire an aggressive, professional sales force–calling mainly on individual advertisers and prospects–to enhance the paper's image with the advertisers. Only 10-25 percent of responding papers' revenues came from advertising directed by agencies; therefore, calling on agencies would not produce much benefit.

The research report ended with the conclusion that the *Edition* "should be successful in this market. There is a strong indication that the *Edition* is needed in Cleveland. . . ." (Business Plan, Cleveland *Edition* 1986: 65). The keys to achieving this success are:

• Maintaining the high quality of editorials
• Providing a clear definition of the audience to advertisers
• Hiring experienced management

- Focusing distribution in a few select areas at first
- Having an aggressive, trained sales force. (Business Plan, Cleveland *Edition* 1986: 66)

The research also pointed out three areas in the plan which needed to be resolved after publication recommenced:

- To charge for the paper or distribute it free
- To use take-out insert sections or not
- To use zoned advertising or total geographic coverage. (Business Plan, Cleveland *Edition* 1986: 66-67)

Interestingly enough, these three concerns reappear throughout the life of *Locus*; they are some of the perennial questions which surround the smaller–particularly weekly suburban–newspapers trying to compete with major metropolitan daily newspapers.

With this survey in hand, management set out to develop an advertising and promotion strategy to carry out the paper's reappearance. The first target of the sales staff was proprietors in and near its distribution points.

> . . . (The) *Edition* sales staff will encourage proprietors of its distribution points to become regular advertisers in the paper. More than any other potential advertiser it is these proprietors that will know best what their customers think about the *Edition*. An empty rack at the end of the week is a certain sign to the proprietor that the paper is a sought-out habit for the reader. Thus, it will be important for the *Edition* distribution manager to monitor closely the positioning of each week's supply of papers in the stores and the distribution and sales managers will work together to coordinate their efforts. (Business Plan, Cleveland *Edition* 1986: 30)

Altogether an admirable plan, it has a feature that I do not approve of: empty racks. I have had extensive discussions with clients and others who publish free circulation periodicals; there seems to be a division of opinion about "empty racks at the end of the week." Some feel, as the staff of the *Edition* did, that an empty rack–and the sooner in the cycle it is empty the better–shows a "hot" publication. Some feel that the publication in the rack–admittedly few by the end of the publishing cycle–stands for quality and represents a free advertisement for the publication. And, of course, no disappointed readers who were unable to pick up the publication. The jury is still out on this point.

Much more damaging, however, is the statement that "(more) than any other potential advertiser it is these proprietors that will know best what their customers think about the *Edition*." This is very true. When the *Edition* hit the streets for the third time, its offices were in the same building as my firm's. The Arcade, built in 1892, has a large, glass-covered "street" of shops and offices five stories high, with large office towers at each end. There are literally dozens of stores, restaurants, and offices, many of which would be prime candidates for advertising in the *Edition* given who the *Edition*'s readers were and the customers these entities seek. On Thursday, the day the *Edition* hit the street, Gunlocke and others from the paper would often stand at the entrances to the Arcade and hand out copies of the paper; everyone at the tables which line the "street" would be reading the *Edition*–and this activity was clearly visible to all in the Arcade. Bill Gunlocke drank his morning coffee in the atrium with owners of many of these establishments on a relatively frequent basis. It says something about the paper's success in telling its story to potential advertisers when these proprietors–many of them friends of Gunlocke and unanimously readers of the paper–rarely advertised. When asked why not, they usually shrugged their shoulders and said that they didn't need the paper–their customers knew them.

Why did the *Edition* fail to tell its story adequately? Did it run afoul of the "Build It and They Will Come" mentality of so many new service providers? Gunlocke's attitude toward advertisers and advertising quoted above shows that such a mentality permeated the organization from the top down. Or was something else at work here? The Chairman of DECOY has always stated that Cleveland is a tough town to start anything new in; that it takes at least three years to establish a new publication and carry it to a true break-even point. The *Edition* never had 36 consecutive months of publication; as the paper passed the 24-month length in early 1992, Gunlocke was at his most optimistic about reaching break-even consistently–

and maybe even making a small profit from time to time. Clearly, the paper's on-and-off-again life operated to deny it a longer life; the survey of other alternative newspapers mentioned consistency of publication as a crucial variable. Although the *Edition* was on the street every Thursday–and usually during the morning rush hour–the fact that it suspended publication from time to time made potential advertisers understandably suspicious that the paper might suspend again.

A second reason for the paper's failure relating to advertisers and potential advertisers was their perception that Cleveland and by extension the advertisers–merchants and "entertainment venues" alike–desperately needed another media outlet because Cleveland was a "one-newspaper town." And they frequently looked to the *Edition* to simply be another outlet. One damning comment from a movie theater owner–and not a typical movie theater owner, but one who was trying to keep a large, old, one-screen theater alive, and not showing mainline, first-run movies in the place–about the advertising rates was the fact that the rates were "the same as for the (suburban chain of weeklies) *Sun* papers; therefore, they were too high for a new paper. You will have a tough time breaking into the movie market without lower rates at first." In the next breath, the owner said that the "papers were picked up like crazy" at his theater.

In fact, it was this seemingly eternal difficulty of potential advertisers to equate the large and intensely loyal readership with potential consumers of their goods and services that doomed the *Edition* from the first. Many potential advertisers were avid readers, and many who were not had seen who the "typical" readers were as they came into their stores and picked up copies of the paper. Nevertheless, they were never able to mentally translate those readers into customers for themselves.

Why not? And were "professionals" from advertising agencies able to do a better job at this task? The *Edition* finally produced a reader survey late in its life; it ran in the paper around 1991, with results which could have been forecast prior to its being conducted. The typical reader was a baby boomer with above-average income, lived in the suburbs but worked downtown, etc. Seemingly a good market for firms who would advertise in such a periodical. Why was the *Edition* unable to turn its readership into a benefit for their advertisers?

This fault does not lie wholly with Gunlocke's disdain for commerce. There were two overarching problems which led to this ongoing difficulty. First was the fact that, although 35,000 copies were printed and distributed every week, the *Edition* never had an audit, so its figures (and survey) were unverifiable. Several respondents from advertising agencies to the Case Western Reserve survey had mentioned that they needed verifiable numbers. And they would have preferred a paid subscription or price per issue for those picked up from racks. Free newspapers do not have the greatest reputation in the world among advertising professionals. And the *Edition* was unable to break through this resistance to unaudited numbers and free subscriptions to show the advertising community–both advertising agency professionals and potential merchant advertisers–that their readers were good customers. Part of this difficulty lay, no doubt, in the astronomical turnover in the sales department, as well as its lack of professionalism. Few merchants ran coupons to verify response; there was no mention of the advisability of such an advertisement in any literature provided to potential advertisers.

But more catastrophic than any of these mechanical and management failures was the fact that the *Edition* was perceived as one kind of paper by its management–and very largely as the same kind of paper by its readers–but another kind of paper by the advertising community of Cleveland. Although no perceptual maps were ever produced, a set of conjectural maps is produced herein as Figure 5.1. One can readily see that although both readers and advertisers viewed the *Edition* as an "alternative" newspaper, what they each meant by "alternative" was quite different. With columnists such as Roldo Bartimole appearing weekly, the *Edition* was seen by the business community as antibusiness. Although this is an unfair characterization of the paper–Gunlocke did not impose an editorial viewpoint on any of his authors–it was a perception that stuck. I do not think readers felt that way about the paper; they mostly were looking for stories that the *Plain Dealer* would not carry.

Because the potential advertisers and advertising professionals wanted the *Edition* to compete with the *Plain Dealer* and the suburban weeklies, the paper got caught in an impossible dilemma. On

FIGURE 5.1. Hypothetical Perceptual Map of the Cleveland *Edition* Comparing Readers with the Advertising Community

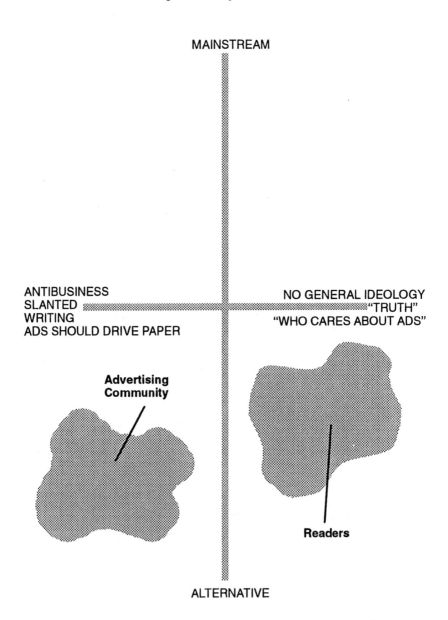

the one hand, it did not have large, verifiable, auditable numbers of paid subscribers to show to advertisers trying to talk in terms of "cost per thousand," and on the other hand, it wanted to keep what was truly a large number of readers who clearly wanted what the *Edition* was providing them.

Unfortunately, these two groups wanted such disparate things from the paper that it was probably impossible for it to keep both groups happy. Unfortunately for the *Edition*'s long-term survival and Gunlocke's pocketbook, it proved easier to give the readers what they wanted than to please the advertisers. And thus the *Edition* failed. In the next chapter we will see what happened when a savvy, experienced publisher focused on one group of advertisers and the paper's readers, while ignoring–for seemingly perfectly good reasons–another group of advertisers.

In late December 1993, I ran into Bill Gunlocke for the first time since that summer; now that he was back teaching English at a Catholic girls' school, he was rarely seen in his usual haunts in the Arcade. When I asked how things were going, he mentioned that he was in the process of launching another publication. This time it was to be sponsored by a "major bookstore chain" and would be a free newspaper of nothing but book reviews. Gunlocke stated that, as he looked around after the *Edition* folded, he realized that when people went into a video store, they knew what videos to rent because there were reviews of videos and movies everywhere–including television. But that there was no easily accessible collection of reviews for someone going into a bookstore to buy a book. This publication was dummied and about to go to prototype early in 1994. Will he have learned from his *Edition* experiences? At least to a certain extent he does seem to have learned: this time it will all be done on a presold basis.

Chapter 6

DECOY, Inc.

Chapters 7 and 8 are both about services developed and marketed by subsidiaries of DECOY, Inc. I will present a capsule history of the firm and to a certain extent its culture, as that is important to a fuller understanding of what was going on with both *Locus* and InfoVision.

DECOY was founded in the late 1950s in northern Ohio, primarily as a weekly newspaper publishing and printing operation; it was among the first to use web-offset and cold type outside the New York City area. In the 1960s DECOY entered the real estate publishing market with *Homes Illustrated,* black-and-white newsprint photographic magazines of homes for sale distributed free to interested homebuyers. By the late 1980s, DECOY was publishing approximately 20 weekly suburban newspapers, 20 *Homes Illustrated* magazines, and one weekly real estate newspaper, covering cities from Southern California to northern Ohio. DECOY has remained a technological innovator in the industry, using laser cameras and digital typesetting equipment. And, in 1977, DECOY began the development of *CompuAd,* a computer program that writes classified advertisements for houses. By the late 1980s several hundred copies of *CompuAd* had been sold in the United States and overseas.

In 1986 DECOY started planning for a reorganization which was to proceed to set up divisions: Real Estate Publishing, to take care of the *Homes Illustrated* publications; Newspaper Publishing, to handle the newspapers and the printing plant at headquarters; Electronic Publishing, to deal with *CompuAd,* its descendents, and Info-Vision; and an incubator to deal with several new ventures that were in process at the time and others which were expected to come in the future. One essential point which was not to change during the reorganization was that DECOY was to remain a corporation whose stock was all held by the founding family; it was held at the time by the founder himself.

The major new venture in process was called Triples, a relocation one-stop service center in Colorado, already a hub for DECOY, with several *Homes Illustrated* magazines published there as well as serving as headquarters for one of the authors of the *CompuAd* program. Persons interested in relocating to Colorado as well as companies relocating large numbers of employees there were expected to avail themselves of several services located in the center: an overview of the area itself, school information, mortgage pre-qualification, doctor referral, etc. InfoVision (then called Home-Sight) was seen as a way to allow these people to view the kinds of housing available in the market before referring them to a real estate firm. Further interest in InfoVision was generated by the seemingly natural link between *CompuAd*'s ability to write dozens of unique advertisements for each listing with a visual database of listings, "publishing" a pseudo *Homes Illustrated* in real time and in color.

The main reason for DECOY's success in two industries is, without a doubt, the Chairman and founder. A graduate of one Ivy League college and holder of a master's degree from another, he put together a successful company. Its success was the result of a combination of hard work, vision, and top people who were not only good at what they did, but also quite complementary to the Chairman. By his own admission not much of an administrator, he has an extremely low threshold of boredom; therefore, his senior people need to be able to pick up his intellectual "dirty clothes" where he has dropped them and carry projects through to their conclusion. He has consistently been able to find such people.

Most of DECOY's innovative posture is also directly attributable to the Chairman. Blessed with a wide-ranging and inquiring mind, he continually has asked questions beginning with "why can't we?" or "why doesn't?"–questions that often lead to innovative solutions to problems. Because he is a Chairman who lets his managers manage, he has no difficulty "taking time from the same old grind" (Berton, 1989) for innovation–in fact, innovation frequently takes precedence over operations, often to the distress of line managers. Thus DECOY fits within Pearson's (1988) five key activities which make some firms very good innovators, despite not having a clear structure or a clear strategic focus. These activities include creating an environment that values performance above all else, structuring to permit innovative ideas to rise above the demands of operations, defining a focus that lets the company channel its innovation realistically, knowing where to look for good ideas, and going after good ideas full speed. With the Chairman leading the innovation and heading the incubator, innovation would continue to be the name of the game at DECOY.

The biggest danger of having the Chairman lead the innovation effort, of course, is that it is difficult to stop a bad idea, particularly when it is the Chairman's own. In fact, Staw (1976), and Staw and Ross (1987a, 1987b; Ross and Staw (1993)), have written extensively on escalation of commitment and its causes; InfoVision will be discussed as an object lesson in such escalation. According to DECOY folklore, *CompuAd* started one day when the Chairman, reacting to the stream of bad advertising copy delivered for *Homes Illustrated* by real estate agents, said, "Can't we get a computer to write this stuff better?" And, in fact, after an investment of several years and hundreds of thousands of dollars, the answer is unequivocally "yes." However, much of the Chairman's time and attention was devoted to the day-to-day task of so doing, to the probable detriment of DECOY. Although *CompuAd,* InfoVision, and other projects clearly fit into the founder's vision for the future of DECOY–a vision he had difficulty articulating–it is questionable if the Chairman of a mid-sized firm should be spending his time debugging software, even if that software is to be the firm's major new product. There are, however, offsetting advantages to having the Chairman lead the innovation effort. First, there can be no higher champion than the Chairman; if the Chairman wants to move, the firm moves. Second, Ronstadt (1988) has shown that entrepreneurial careers are longer if the entrepreneur launches at least a second venture.

The culture of DECOY in 1986 could only be described as open. (For details about the culture and an attempt to change it, see Susbauer, Cahill, Warshawsky, and Beckman [1994].) The Chairman and other managers were readily accessible to everyone in the company. Further, there was little structure and almost no written job descriptions among senior managers. The concept of "corporate staff with portfolios" did not exist, so almost anyone could be assigned to any special project–matrix management by default. The individual newspaper and magazine operations were highly autonomous, with next-to-no formal reporting requirements from the manager to the Chairman. Except for financial data, the only reporting consisted of telephone conversations, usually initiated by the Chairman when he wished to know "what's going on." Failure was rarely punished by termination; after 30 years in business, the Chairman was proud to announce that he had fired only two people. Displeasure was, instead, evidenced by a noticeable coolness in relations with the Chairman. People were intensely loyal to the Chairman; when a program of awarding service pins was initiated in 1989, several 20-year pins were given to relatively low-level employees.

A striking feature of the firm's culture was the fact that none of the entities identified itself as "A DECOY Company" until many months or even years after the introduction of that name. All the entities were known by their own names, and most of their local advertisers–and most of the advertisers for all the entities were local–thought the publications locally owned. The DECOY name was introduced, appeared on the mastheads of some (but by no means all) of the publications, and no general explanation of what DECOY was or why the name was being changed was made to either advertisers or employees.

Since DECOY was in two quite different industries–newspapers and real estate publishing–there was no common language across the industries. Their only commonality was that both products were printed on newsprint. In one division the customers were almost exclusively real estate firms and their agents; in the other, customers were mostly retailers and individual subscribers. Both newspaper managers and *Homes Illustrated* managers had a good feel for what their advertisers wanted and needed, but used different terminology to articulate that feel to corporate staff. Communication as a cultural performance (Pacanowsky and O'Donnell-Trujillo, 1983) was difficult to decipher in these circumstances as there were multiple subcultures (if not true multiple cultures) within the firm. Thus corporate staff wound up with a confused sense of who DECOY's customers were. This was not auspicious for continued long-term success (Miller, 1987) as the 1980s drew to a close.

Chapter 7

Locus

When the Cleveland *Press* ceased publication, the real estate community in Cleveland almost immediately felt the icy blast of monopoly power breathing down its neck–or at least thought that it did. Although there was no longer a competing daily paper, as mentioned in Chapter 5, there were plenty of media outlets which competed with the *Plain Dealer* for real estate advertising dollars: two chains of suburban weeklies, daily papers from outlying communities entering Cuyahoga County, plus a biweekly *Homes* magazine, similar to *Homes Illustrated*. Clearly there was media competition to the *Plain Dealer* for the real estate advertising dollar, just as there was for the entertainment advertising dollar which the *Edition* felt it needed so badly. But the owners of the two largest real estate firms in Cleveland nervously expected the *Plain Dealer* to raise advertising rates, so they approached the Chairman of DECOY, Inc., with a proposition: he would publish a real estate paper in Cleveland with support (and co-ownership) of the principals of the two firms.

The Chairman was intrigued with the proposition. Although DECOY was headquartered in a town that was only 50 miles from Cleveland, so the location would not be difficult from a logistical standpoint. Further, the Chairman and his wife maintained a *pied à terre* in Cleveland and were socially active in the city–both of them were on boards of trustees of theater and other arts organizations. Moreover, a competitor in the real estate publishing industry that DECOY personnel considered to be a difficult competitor published a *Homes* magazine in town. And, last, the Chairman was concerned that with the rise of the baby boom generation and beyond, the demand for black-and-white newsprint publications for houses for sale would decline, and he was looking for an opportunity to publish something with more pizzazz–more color, more editorial content, more of a real estate newspaper that would cover the market and be a newspaper for both realtors and those interested in houses. Further, this new publication might present DECOY with a good opportunity to capture an advertising market that the *Homes Illustrated* format never did: the so-called aftermarket (carpet companies, carpenters, aluminum siding firms, etc.), none of whom regularly advertised in *Homes Illustrated*.

As a prelude to making the decision to proceed, the Chairman went to Toronto, Ontario, in 1984 to scout out a real estate publication there that he thought could serve as a model for what he had in mind. His entourage for the trip included his Senior Corporate Vice President–who doubled as production manager and general troubleshooter for all the publications–and Miriam Shapiro, the editor of one of his Cleveland newspapers, who was to become *Locus*'s editorial director, and–until her death in 1988–one of the Chairman's most trusted sounding boards. The Toronto newspaper was bright and colorful and well-filled with advertisements; the trip seemed to show that such a publication could be produced successfully and be introduced successfully into a crowded market.

When the team returned home, three distinct research efforts were undertaken: production feasibility, editorial copy, and financial viability. Production feasibility was the easiest of the three research projects. Given the state of the production and press facilities at DECOY's plant, it would be possible for DECOY to undertake all the prepress functions, but printing a large color newspaper was beyond its capabilities–printing would have to be farmed out. But a local newspaper had excess capacity at its printing plant and could handle the printing job for *Locus*.

Editorial copy for the projected newspaper proved to be no problem. J. D. Wallace, a nationally known real estate writer–and the Chairman's sister–was named National Editor and produced a memo outlining what the editorial content of the publication should be once the paper was produced (Wallace, 1984):

LOCUS STARTS WITH A POSITIVE, BREATHTAKING THESIS . . . that in the resale-home business, we are witnessing

THE RECYCLING OF AMERICA . . . let's take the rehab trend as a true one that will last into the 90s . . . and ride it, shape it . . . encourage it . . . make people feel good about it . . . dedicate ourselves editorially to it. After all, that's where the space is, that's where the established, close-in neighborhood possibilities are . . . all mixed with the joys of "building," through rebuilding.

There then followed 19 pages of story ideas and column thoughts that would lead from the thesis stated above. *Locus* was born with a clear editorial mission–like the *Edition* it was to be distinctively different from anything that was currently on Cleveland's streets. And none of this so much as mentioned the section for house-for-sale advertisements that was the entire *raison d'être* of the paper! The fact that almost none of these ideas was ever produced should not detract from the import of this memo. There was a tremendous amount of material available to craft a newspaper *which would get readers* who were interested in real estate–or home decoration or real estate law as it applied to property owners, etc., etc.– apart from those individuals who would pick up the publication because they wanted to see the house-for-sale ads. This was deemed to be crucial to the long-term health of the paper.

DECOY's accounting firm was asked to prepare *pro forma* financial statements for the company in creation and, in June 1984, it complied. Management's assumptions, while rosy (they always are in *pro formas*)

. . . provide a reasonable basis for management's forecast. However, some assumptions inevitably will not materialize and unanticipated events and circumstances may occur; therefore, the actual results achieved during the forecast period will vary from the forecast, and the variations may be material. (*Locus, Inc.*, 1984)

This is the standard, American Institute of Certified Public Accountant's language on *pro forma* statements; how material the results achieved were to vary from the forecast will be seen as the story unfolds in this chapter.

Based upon the successful results of these three separate but interrelated research efforts, the Chairman decided to go ahead with the project, now seen as a newspaper. During the summer of 1984 some of DECOY's management met with John Nottingham and Darby Scott, both of Nottingham-Spirk Design Associates, a Cleveland industrial design firm, to discuss design criteria for both the paper and the street distribution boxes that would be used. At a lunch at "That Place on Bellflower," the paper became known as *Splash!*–a name which, fortunately, did not last long. Colors and typefaces were quickly decided upon–both created by Darby Scott. The paper was to be a broadsheet (regular newspaper size) for the editorial section, wrapped around a removable tabloid section devoted exclusively to the houses-for-sale advertisements. The distribution boxes were to be a warm red with dark-red plastic house-roofs. Nottingham-Spirk would design and fabricate the tops, and contract with a conventional newspaper-box supplier for the boxes themselves. Everything concerned with the paper itself and its physical presence on the street was to be unique but duplicable, as the Chairman was hoping to create in Cleveland a prototype for a news medium that could be rolled out in cities around the country.

The business portion of *Locus* also needs some explanation. The company which would publish the paper was structured as a corporation DECOY was to manage, with shareholders from DECOY and the two largest real estate brokerage firms in town; no real secret was made of this fact. The two real estate firms signed contracts with the publishing company, each guaranteeing to place at least a middle-six-figure amount of advertising in the ensuing 12 months. An attractive office was opened in a restored late-nineteenth century office building in a resurgent area of town. By late 1984, the paper was in business, and the first issue was on the street.

Locus was an immediate hit with readers. Almost instantly distribution hit 35,000 copies per week, and all but the merest handful were scooped up as soon as the paper hit the racks. Although DECOY's Chairman avoided publicity about the project, and thus there were few articles about *Locus* in Cleveland's many publications, it was talked about on the street and among realtors.

In an effort to better understand its readers, *Locus* commissioned National Market Measures to conduct a focus group in February

1985, with two general purposes: to understand how *Locus* was perceived in the market, and to understand better the process of house shopping. Ten individuals who had actively been in the real estate market within the past two years met at NMM's facility on February 4. The relevant results of the focus group were quickly summarized: readers liked the paper, although some of the people had seen the paper but, for one reason or another, had not picked it up. The paper was seen as filling an information gap between the daily paper and the *Homes* magazine of which people were quite aware; it offered better organized and more descriptive listings which were more informative and more appealing–but it contained too few listings when compared with its competitors.

In June 1985, *Locus* commissioned National Market Measures to undertake a readership survey to provide some quantitative feedback to management, and a reader profile to potential advertisers (NMM, 1985b). This study had been contemplated when the focus group was commissioned and was considered the second part of the same research effort. The firm conducted 250 intercept interviews, 25 at each of ten locations where the paper was distributed, geographically dispersed throughout the paper's distribution area. This is the kind of readership survey which free-to-the-reader newspapers need to do to establish credibility with the advertising profession. Rather than some insert which is to be mailed back (and whose results can be manipulated by one individual or small group who obtain a large percentage of the reply questionnaires), an intercept survey is more "quantitatively" respectable, if designed properly. A survey of 250 individuals out of a circulation base of 35,000 may not sound like much, but it is a large enough sample to be reasonably valid.

The survey generated some interesting findings beyond the usual demographic information. One of the questions asked was, of course, "What is your main reason for picking up *Locus* today?" Forty-two percent said that they were in the market for a house or apartment; 39 percent said that they were interested in learning more about real estate, mortgage options, interest rates, and house prices in general. Thirty-seven percent said that the paper was informative, easy-to-read; and 17 percent said that it caught their eye, was colorful, and attention-getting–in short, that the paper was attractive enough visually to entice them to pick it up, even if they had no "real" reason to be interested in a real estate newspaper. This point should not be lost; many of the Chairman's friends, who would never be in the market for a house, continually told him that they looked forward to picking up the paper every week and reading it from one end to the other–not including the listings. Some of the verbatim comments elicited by the survey are interesting, particularly in light of the paper's later history (NMM, 1985b):

> It's become a habit. . . .This paper gives me insight about rental apartments and home sales, especially locations and prices.

> We already own two homes so we enjoy reading the home improvement articles.

> The color caught my eye. The pictures on the front page were attention-getting. The titles of the articles sounded interesting.

> The attractive colors on the front page caught my attention. It looked very similar to *USA Today* [this was a deliberate design decision]. I'm looking for a house, and I figured that this paper could show me what's available.

> It's free. I want to see what the real estate market is like. I'm thinking about going into real estate sales.

> I saw the pictures of the pretty house on the front page, and I wanted to read about it.

Although *Locus* was a hit with its readers, it was not a hit with its advertisers. The two largest firms met their commitments to advertise in the amounts specified, but the rest of the real estate firms in Cleveland were reluctant to advertise in *Locus*. One of the reasons most often given to the sales force was the fact that the rest of the real estate community knew who the shareholders of the paper were, and did not want to spend advertising dollars to enrich their competition–perhaps a rational explanation.

But a much more damaging lack of advertising dollars materialized from an unexpected direction: within the two large firms themselves. In the mid-1980s in Cleveland, the individual agents carried a lot of weight about which properties were to be advertised, to what extent they would be advertised, and where those advertisements were to appear, primarily because the advertising dollars came out of the agents' pockets.

There was a tremendous reluctance on the part of individual agents to advertise in *Locus* for two reasons. First, an ad in *Locus* cost more than an ad in the *Homes* magazine and reached fewer people than an ad in the *Plain Dealer*. Second, *Locus* was seen as being a hobby horse of the firms' owners, and the agents were reluctant to line their employers' pockets. *Locus* never was able to explain to the agents why advertisements in the paper cost more than an ad in the *Homes* magazine, and that reaching 600,000 people through the *Plain Dealer* was meaningless if only 30,000 were looking for a house that week. (This is not an easy concept to sell under the best of circumstances; numbers always impress advertisers, even when they *know* that the numbers do not mean anything real.) Agents liked the less-costly advertisements in the *Homes* magazine, even though they realized that the ad was smaller than an ad for the same house would be in *Locus*. Although the focus group participants had stated that they liked the more descriptive ads in *Locus,* such verbiage is anathema to many real estate professionals: "Too many adjectives."

The other source of advertising *Locus* was supposed to attract, never materialized to any great extent either: the aftermarket advertisers. Efforts were made to attract roofers, gutter installers, aluminum siding firms, etc., all without a great deal of success. Most of these firms tend to be relatively small and relatively local in the markets they serve, and *Locus*–despite having numbers that were very small by comparison to the *Plain Dealer*–distributed too many copies over too wide a geographic area for most of the aftermarket companies that had been expected to advertise. When larger, more dispersed firms were solicited–Sherwin-Williams Paint Company (headquartered a few hundred yards from *Locus*'s office), Sears, Roebuck & Co., and others of the same type and size–*Locus*'s distribution numbers were deemed too small for these firms to consider. And so the aftermarket dollars never lived up to expectations.

For the paper's entire life, it staggered on; under-revenued, and over-read, clearly a newspaper–like the *Edition*–whose readers loved it and could not wait for it to appear each week, but just as clearly a newspaper that the advertisers stayed away from in droves.

Significantly, the Chairman knew very early that the paper was in trouble. As early as the February 1985 focus group, consideration was given to redesigning the tabloid listings section to bring it more into line with what the focus group members said they wanted, with minimal display of realtor name associated with a particular property. When the real estate community objected, the design change was scrapped in favor of allowing almost any advertisement format on any tabloid page. Some time later, the broadsheet wrap disappeared altogether and listings were run at the end of what was now just a tabloid newspaper.

Despite the changes, realtors still did not rush to advertise in *Locus*. The lack of realtor advertising was noticeable; and almost the only realtor ads were from the two guaranteeing firms, although one small independent firm loved *Locus* from the beginning and spent a disproportionate amount of its advertising budget there, taking it away from the *Homes* magazine. The only thing that kept the paper going–other than the sheer will of the Chairman–was advertising by new home builders.

DECOY, Inc., had long operated on the premise that realtors hated to advertise, for a host of reasons (Wallace, 1985). Real estate agents were vain, loved to see their name in print (and the name of the firm), but resented having to spend money to advertise a particular property. The only reason most agents advertised a property was "seller pressure"; sellers wanted to see activity on their property, knew that people who are looking for a house look at the ads, and complained to their listing agent that their house was not getting any play. (How true this perception was may be questioned; however, a recent book by a real estate consulting firm recommends that agents choose the firm that they intend to go with, in part, based upon how much advertising is done by the firm and its agents–not a mention about selling houses [Dooley and Dahlheimer, 1989].) Further, a study commissioned by DECOY found that the only variable which explained differences in the speed with which a house sold was length of continuous advertising; although the results were sketchy, preliminary, never followed up, and the data upon which the conclusion was based was in part questionable, it confirmed DECOY's impression of what worked and of the "stupidity" of real estate agents.

New house builders, however, were another story. Builders operate more like businesspeople than real estate agents do. They have inventory which costs them money; they realize that every day a house sits unsold costs them interest expense on the construction loan they have taken out to build the house. Therefore, builders will advertise–and advertise lavishly if they have a new development they are trying to sell rather than one house in an established neighborhood. Because *Locus* was widely read and well known, the builders started advertising; at first, just a builder here and there, and very occasionally. But soon, more and more builders advertised more and more often. I remember the Chairman telling me at one point–I cannot be sure of the date, but it was before the builders had become important advertisers in *Locus*–that his experience with the *Homes Illustrated* magazines was that one had to be very careful about letting the builders into a real estate publication or they would quickly take it over and drive out the resale house ads–the mainstay of the realtors. And then, when economic conditions turned on the builders, they would fold and the realtors would not come back quickly into the publication, leaving the publication vulnerable to failure.

By the middle of 1987 the builders had basically taken over the advertising space in *Locus*. Several builders routinely took full-page ads. As the Chairman had forecast, it then became more difficult to solicit realtor ads for resale houses as *Locus* became known in the trade as a new house publication. This probably truly marked the beginning of the end of the paper, although it lasted for three more years. Never again was there much optimism about *Locus*'s long-term survival. Never again was there talk about taking the *Locus* concept nationwide. Never again was there talk about *Locus* becoming profitable. The only thought for *Locus* was to get to break-even and then examine the available options.

The first step toward getting the paper to break-even was to reduce costs. Several steps were taken: reducing editorial staff and changing some of the personnel to reduce salary expense. When the lease on the office space came up for renewal in early 1989, the office was moved to the basement of the local Builders Industry Association offices–redoubling the paper's identification as a "builders' rag" in the minds of the few real estate agents who paid attention. To show what chaos had descended upon the operation, some of the furniture was to be moved to the DECOY headquarters in Sandusky; the mover hired by the paper's general manager was not licensed to leave Cuyahoga County and, therefore, could not complete the move they had contracted. By moving to the BIA building, a tremendous savings in rent was achieved. Further, the Chairman moved away, to offices in the Old Arcade–thus staying downtown and physically distancing himself from *Locus*–a fact not lost on *Locus*'s personnel who now rarely saw him. The number of copies printed was reduced, lowering the cost of production, although not very much. In short, by early 1989, *Locus* was clearly dying.

At the National Association of Realtors convention in November 1988, the Chairman had first broached the subject of what to do with the paper. Recommendations were sought from JoAnn Dennis, the Chief Financial Officer of DECOY, and several others, including me. After joint analysis of the prospects and finances, Dennis and I both voted to kill the paper quickly and cleanly, and as soon as possible. This was not done. In September 1989, the Chairman broached the idea of selling the paper to a company in Cleveland composed of former *Locus* employees who had left to buy an advertising publication in the boating industry. A deal was quickly outlined, but the Chairman refused to go forward. Finally, in March 1990, *Locus* suspended publication, after draining off a tremendous amount of the Chairman's time and attention, as well as that of many other DECOY personnel. DECOY was freed to pursue other projects which had potential to become profitable, a potential *Locus* clearly lacked by this time.

What went wrong with *Locus?* In 1987 and 1988, DECOY had been solicited and entered negotiations to publish an automobile newspaper in a small Ohio city which was a one-newspaper town. In 1986, the Cleveland Automobile Dealers Association had also approached the Chairman with the thought of his publishing such a newspaper for them. A competing chain of suburban weeklies got the job, at great expense and complete embarrassment to all when *Sun Wheels* failed completely after only a few weeks. DECOY, however, achieved some recognition by entering the fray with some innovative concepts. When the dealers' association in the other city was looking for an alternative, they quickly called on DECOY.

As DECOY got further into negotiations, the Chairman asked me to outline a business plan for the venture. As part of that process, and because much of this venture was going to be patterned upon DECOY's experience with *Locus,* I interviewed several key people in the *Locus* start-up. The key question I asked was "What did you do wrong at the start of *Locus?*" as I didn't want to repeat any errors. Nine errors were mentioned by the Chairman and/or Miriam Shapiro.

1. The introduction was strung out too long.

2. We didn't feel the need for a strong leader, and the project manager didn't work out. This was supposed to be an automatic winner, given the guarantees.

3. We weren't prepared for the initial outpouring of ads from the realtors; this led to an emotional letdown on their part when we couldn't deliver what we had sold them.

4. We used salaried salespeople because of the feeling that it would all be house accounts; we never sold down past the owners to the branch office managers and agents.

5. We didn't put a circulation manager on soon enough.

6. We focused sales effort on the after market too soon; more lead time was needed to get the product accepted (and then we never really followed through with these advertisers again).

7. We were overstaffed and misstaffed and over-overheaded.

8. We overestimated revenues badly.

9. We didn't start out with a big enough run of papers; we should have started at 80,000 copies per week instead of 35,000. It is always easy to cut the run, but often quite difficult to raise the run significantly.

Nowhere on this list of "could haves" and "should haves" is any indication that *Locus* suffered from problems with the Marketing Concept or with acceptance of the paper because it did not fill a need on the part of the readers or advertisers. Yet I would propose, which was not possible in the interview with the Chairman, that the real reason for *Locus*'s demise was its lack of fit with the advertisers; they saw no need for the publication–just like the *Edition*. And, further, given the mindset and years of experience of DECOY personnel prior to the launch of the paper, this lack of fit could have been foreseen.

As mentioned above, DECOY personnel did not have a flattering view of real estate agents, or their understanding of house buyers and what they wanted. In fact, several realtors were invited to watch the February 1985, focus group; they heard these individuals complain bitterly about real estate agents as a group and their inability to make buyers happy. All of an agent's attention is focused upon the seller; they work for the seller. But until a buyer is found, the house (obviously) cannot sell, and the agent cannot receive the commission. This is so patently obvious that it has always bewildered DECOY personnel that realtors do not seem to understand this fact (or understand it in the same way that DECOY personnel do)–they are dependent upon buyers in order to make a living by selling real estate. Realtors continue to lavish all their attention and understanding upon sellers.

At one time, the Chairman asked a man whom he considers to be the brightest realtor he knows what would be the perfect sale. Dick responded: "Selling a listing I got yesterday to someone I showed it to today. That way I have almost no expenses, I don't have to split the commission with anyone, and everyone's happy." The Chairman did not press Dick to find out how he expected to sell the house the day after getting a listing; without advertising it, such a sale is normally unlikely.

Seeing *Locus* not as a newspaper but as an advertising medium is the key to understanding its ultimate failure. A clear success with readers–in fact I still hear about it from time to time despite its being dead for four years–it failed with the real estate agents. Why? There are three reasons which strike me as arresting in this regard.

First was the fact that the real estate agents perceived no gap in the services offered them by established print media. Between the *Plain Dealer,* the *Homes* magazine, and the suburban weeklies, everyone who wanted to advertise in print had an opportunity to do so. If one does not have a great belief in the efficacy of advertising to sell houses, as DECOY perceived that most realtors did not (DECOY, 1986a), does it matter if the house gets two lines in the Sunday *Plain Dealer* classifieds, or a 1″ × 2″ (with photograph) display ad in the *Homes* magazine? Unlikely. The ads are there if the owner of the house begins to pressure the real estate agent about why the property is not selling. If *Locus* appears on the scene with better advertising copy (much of it written by *CompuAd*) and bigger pages with the opportunity for more copy and bigger, clearer pictures, so what? It also appeared with higher advertising rates than the *Homes* magazine and smaller circulation than the *Plain Dealer*– so it entered the market in the always-dreaded middle.

This lack of perceived need for a new black-and-white newsprint medium on the part of agents did not extend to either color magazines–a couple of which were started in the Cleveland market during *Locus*'s lifetime, aimed at "upscale buyers of prestige homes"– or television shows of listings. Although a thorough discussion of either of these media is beyond the scope of this book (a short discussion of real estate television is in Chapter 8), agents were being asked to pay for having their "better" listings appear on these shows at the same time that *Locus* was trying to get their advertising dollar. To many agents it must have seemed as though rather than needing an alternative to the daily paper, Cleveland needed *fewer* advertising media.

A second fact was that the champions of the paper were also the owners of the two largest real estate brokerage firms in town. Had this fact not been known outside the boardrooms, it might have been different. But the smaller agencies were reluctant to advertise because any profit from their advertising in the paper would accrue to their competitors. They might have feared being squeezed out by these two firms which could afford to buy whole pages in the *Plain Dealer* on Sunday and thus might be interested in buying whole pages in *Locus* with its lower rates. We found some of the same reluctance in the abortive automobile paper discussed briefly above.

But just as reluctant were agents who worked for these two firms. Some of this reluctance might be the result of the "normal" antipathy between boss and worker, even though the legal relationship in much of the real estate industry is between corporation and independent contractor. More of the reluctance came, I think, from structural changes occurring in the real estate industry at the same time *Locus* existed. The industry was heading more and more to full-time agents, more of whom were, in effect, renting desk space and other items from the firm and keeping their entire commission check rather than earning a piece of the commission and having the firm pick up the tab for everything. These agents were called "100 Percenters" in recognition of their compensation scheme. An entire company–Re-Max Inc.–franchising offices nationwide and causing some widespread distress, was gaining real strength just at this time. If the agents were going to have to start paying for advertising directly out of their pockets, they were going to be more skeptical; just because something was pushed by headquarters was no reason why they would have to like it. And the fact that DECOY never "sold through" to the agents, explaining why *Locus* would be a good buy for them, generating more sales leads than the *Plain Dealer,* the *Homes* magazine, or the suburban weeklies, did not make life easier for the paper.

Third, a list in the *Edition's* research mentioned in Chapter 4 as unresolved items, was also unresolved by *Locus* (Business Plan, Cleveland *Edition,* 1986: 66-67):

- To charge for the paper or distribute it free
- To use take-out insert sections or not
- To use zoned advertising or total geographic coverage

The fact that zoned advertising was not made available in *Locus* made it difficult to sell the paper to the smaller, aftermarket companies, as mentioned above. Further, without zoned coverage in a city which is geographically split like Cleveland, realtors on one side of town frequently complained that they were paying for readers on the other side of town who would never move across the Cuyahoga River; the *Homes* magazine was split between an east side book and a west side book and thus offered lower rates based upon lower circulation figures on each book.

Inserts were a perennial problem in *Locus*. Originally banned because of production difficulties, inserts were discouraged even after these difficulties were overcome. Inserts probably would have been a vehicle to get do-it-yourself retailers and firms like Sherwin-Williams into the paper, given its small circulation, but these inserts would have offered *Locus* little or no profitability since the advertisers would only have paid a small per-item insertion charge. Producing inserts for advertisers was potentially more lucrative, but only rarely did one appear in the paper, and then only after the builders had come in, since they used inserts the most.

There never was any serious consideration given to charging for *Locus*. Despite having been asked to produce the paper as a counter to the *Plain Dealer*–which as a daily paper, of course, carries a cover price–*Locus*'s competition was normally seen as the *Homes* magazine, which was free. Just before *Locus*'s demise, research was undertaken in-house as to the feasibility of producing a real estate publication bearing a cover price, but such a publication–produced briefly in a trial in 1990–was not *Locus,* nor anything like it. *HomeQuest* was more like *Homes Illustrated,* although it carried with it some of the lessons so painfully and expensively learned through DECOY's experience with *Locus.*

A postscript on *Locus* and trying to make a go of a real estate newspaper in Cleveland recently occurred. The Cleveland Area Board of Realtors decided, at the end of 1993, that its members were paying too much for advertising properties, and that there were too many negative stories about real estate, real estate firms, and real estate agents. In an attempt to counter these problems, the Board of Realtors hired a consultant to investigate some possible solutions to deal with the situation. Early in 1994, it was indicated that the probable solution was going to be a Board-sponsored publication. I hope the consultant that the Board hired not only researched the *Locus* experience, but also did some research in perceptual mapping of real estate agents and other potential advertisers, as well as the potential readers of the publication–but I have no real expectation that this was done.

One last media case follows. It built upon all of DECOY's experience with real estate publishing, yet tried to catch the wave of new technology and the excitement of getting away from the black-and-white printed page. InfoVision was yet another example of trying to squeeze a new service into a crowded market which was unsure whether the service was even desirable.

Chapter 8

Industrializing Services for an Advantage: InfoVision

THE SERVICE

InfoVision is an integrated system consisting of a personal computer, super-high-resolution monitor, and a printer. The system has the capability of dealing with a large data base of real estate classified listings, including both the text for advertising them as well as photographs of the property. By the end of 1988, the program could write ads "on the fly"–in real time–and display several photographs of a single property in a planned sequence, allowing the viewer to take a "tour" through the house. The viewer controlled all this interactively through a touchscreen which required no computer literacy on the viewer's part.

Levitt (1976), in his article entitled "The Industrialization of Service," states that there are three methods to industrialize services: hard, soft (operating procedures), and hybrid technologies. InfoVision is a hybrid technology in which hardware and software are combined with a specific operating procedure to *standardize* the process of obtaining listings and qualifying prospects in the real estate industry–operations which now are performed only to the level of competence of the individual agent or firm. InfoVision is a forward-looking item: it is an attempt to enable real estate firms to exert more control over the selling process by standardizing the interaction of agents and clients, and thus to increase productivity in an industry which has, to date, seemed to care little for that concept.

At this point, a fuller description of the residential real estate market than was presented in Chapter 7 is in order. It is huge in terms of annual dollar volume, number of transactions, number of firms, number of agents, etc. Nevertheless, it is a highly fragmented market with the largest firm, Coldwell Banker (a subsidiary of Sears, Roebuck & Co.), Century 21, a franchisor, and others having a small share of the total market. The number of people employed in the industry is unknown as a large percentage of agents are part-timers. The National Association of Realtors, one of the trade associations, claimed 749,257 members as of 1988; the weekly newspaper which is sent to all its members had a June 1989, audited circulation of 784,230 (NAR, 1989). It is an agency business, where the agents work on behalf of the sellers of property. Therefore, it is one in which the sellers' priorities should mean much more than those of the buyers.

What do sellers want and expect? They want a quick sale at or near their asking price. They expect that their house will be widely advertised. It is at this point that the expectations of the seller deviate from the goals of the seller's agent, for advertising is an expense to the agent whether the house sells or not. Real estate agents, therefore, have an incentive to do as little advertising as possible and, in fact, often have to be bullied by the seller to adver-tise at all (DECOY, 1986a). This conflict seems to be a point of contention between sellers and agents (National Market Measures, 1985a). What do buyers want and expect? They want to see on paper everything available in their price range–not just in the loca-tion they have told the agent they wanted–and then to have the agent show them only what they want (National Market Measures, 1985a). What do the broker/owners of real estate firms want and expect? They want the listings held by their firms shown and sold first as this increases their revenue; they earn their share of the commission for both selling and buying the property. And they, too, want their listings sold quickly.

InfoVision would seem to fit well into the wants and expectations of all the parties mentioned above, with benefits that have not been specified because the industry seems not to recognize the need, such as increasing agent productivity. InfoVision meets the seller's wants and expectations because it advertises the house continuous-ly–in fact, the software continuously shows all the listings in the data base randomly when no one is actively searching. InfoVision meets the agent's wants by prequalifying potential buyers through a financing software module showing users how big a mortgage they may qualify for. InfoVision meets the buyer's wants by allowing buyers to see every available house rather than the agent's selected property list. And, perhaps most important, it meets the broker/owner's wants by making it possible to show the firm's listings first to each viewer, increasing the probability of having the viewers decide that those are the houses they wish to see. And, as an aside, InfoVision can substantially reduce the amount of time agents spend out on the road showing houses to prospects by reducing the number of properties which must be shown physically. This could be a major consideration for real estate firms in areas where traffic congestion is a major problem.

HISTORY OF INFOVISION

InfoVision started in 1985 as the concept of AJH, husband of the manager of one of the Colorado *Homes Illustrated*'s. He saw that there could be a better way of delivering the information to the consumer–interactive, in color, and delivered to the mall where the consumer was spending large amounts of time. He foresaw one of these machines in every mall in the country, linked together electronically, delivering information to consumers for a fee. However, he had no capital and limited access to realtors to get listings. He was a technical visionary, but did not know the real estate market. His wife then approached the Chairman to see if he had any interest. The concept immediately intrigued him and he started a new venture–originally called VideoData–to work on the machines.

The first problem with InfoVision occurred at inception. The Chairman had started numerous ventures in the past with the same formula: he established a new venture and funded it, and the idea person "sweat in" equity until he owned 50 percent. The Chairman kept hands off and allowed the other person to manage. Usually the idea person would be able to manage the operation with help from the very small DECOY corporate staff. In AJH, the Chairman had found a visionary who could not manage. It was a couple of years before this problem showed up as a major concern.

VideoData was a hardware/software integration, storing digitized color photographs of properties on magnetic discs, to allow instant updating of listings. The user in the mall interacted with the machine by using a touchscreen rather than a keyboard, so there was no need for users to think that they were using a computer. The information about the property–number of rooms, number of stories, features, etc.–was stored in a database that could be accessed by the *CompuAd* program which would write advertising copy for the property. In 1985, many parts of this system were expensive: VideoData was on the cutting edge of technology at that time. The computer being used was a clone of the IBM PC/XT with 640 kilobytes of memory–at that time, an expensive proposition. The photographs were "captured" and input with the predecessor of the AT&T Targa system; in 1985, this equipment was also very expensive. The touchscreen user-interface alone cost approximately $1,500 per machine at the time. All of these items led to a cost per machine of approximately $10,000. And herein lay problem number two: cost. With a fixed cost of $10,000, the price per listing to the real estate agent was larger than the typical listing charge in *Homes Illustrated,* albeit on VideoData it was for the life of the listing whereas in *Homes Illustrated* it was for each issue–usually biweekly. AJH had every intention of keeping VideoData at the cutting edge of technology, building in capabilities for laser-disc hookups, and telephone-modem servicing and data entry.

In early 1986, a Coldwell Banker affiliate in Fort Collins, Colorado, agreed to have a machine installed in its booth in the Foothills regional shopping mall on a test basis. By this time the system was called HomeSight and was reasonably similar to its final configuration, although there were further software improvements made later. The system proved to be well received in the test. Initially, the agents who were in the booth with it worried about people's reaction to the system; after a very short period of time, agents *wanted* to be in the booth–an unusual phenomenon. The system proved to be a traffic stopper and a good method for prequalifying prospects, generating listings, getting people to talk to the agents; in short, HomeSight did what it was supposed to do. It attracted buyers, it attracted sellers who wanted *their* house to be on the system, it got men to look at listings–traditionally a difficult proposition for realtors–it enabled the firm to increase market share, it sold more of its own listings, and it increased agent productivity (DECOY, 1986b).

The Foothills test market was a great success. Still, there was one small point that seemed to get overlooked in the excitement: no one from the company paid for a single listing, nor any of the cost of the machine. DECOY thus entered the crucial phase of developing the system without a key datum—what was HomeSight worth to potential customers.

Based on the success of Foothills, negotiations were undertaken with Coldwell Banker's corporate staff in Newport Beach, California, for either another test or a national installation of HomeSight. DECOY considered Coldwell a logical prospect for HomeSight to DECOY for four reasons. First, Coldwell had the most offices under a single ownership of any real estate firm in the country; HomeSight would allow Coldwell to tie the operations together through data interchange. Second, one area that always interests realtors is the relocation market; HomeSight could allow someone moving from Baltimore to Chicago to go to a Coldwell office in Baltimore to discuss selling the current house and at the same time see what was available in Chicago—naturally, the Coldwell Chicago listings. This fact makes it possible for Coldwell to get four transactions from a single seller instead of two: buyer and seller in Baltimore as well as buyer and seller in Chicago. This would represent a vast increase in agent productivity. Third, Coldwell had offices inside Sears stores in addition to its freestanding offices; HomeSight would allow the offices inside the stores a boost in visibility and ability to do business. And fourth, the large size of Coldwell attracted DECOY's attention. DECOY could leverage its success in HomeSight for several purposes: sell the *CompuAd* program for advertisement writing to Coldwell for its entire operation, sell Coldwell on increasing the amount of advertising its offices were taking in *Homes Illustrated,* and start new publications for Coldwell. At the end of 1986 negotiations were successfully concluded for a test market to take place in Tampa, Florida, in early 1987.

Why Tampa? DECOY had no operations in Tampa, nor even in Florida; in fact, the closest operation was *Homes Illustrated* magazine in Ohio. DECOY accepted the Tampa test market for two reasons. First, the Chairman and AJH were too eager to get started, to get the test underway and prove that HomeSight worked. Second, AJH was overconfident about his ability to solve the problems that would inevitably arise. Fort Collins was a short drive from the AJH headquarters; Tampa was hours away by airplane. Both the overeagerness and overconfidence were to prove troublesome during the test.

Coldwell wanted Tampa for three reasons. First, many of their offices in the Tampa area were based in Sears stores; Coldwell thought this would be a good opportunity to see if HomeSight could deliver in those circumstances. Second, Tampa was remote from Sears's Chicago headquarters and Coldwell's Newport Beach headquarters; this would allow for more hands-off testing then Colorado did. Third, many Sears executives wintered in Tampa allowing them to get a visiting-fireman's tour of HomeSight and be kept abreast of the latest ideas.

The actual test in Tampa did not go well at all. Many changes had occurred between what had been contemplated and what was actually done. The first two of these were probably fatal. First, the geographical extent of the market was expanded tremendously to include six malls, including one in Sarasota. Second, because of the presence of another real estate firm in the malls themselves, HomeSight machines could not actually be in the mall; they had to be in the Sears store near the Coldwell space. HomeSight was originally designed to stop traffic, but there was not much traffic to stop in these locations. Third, Coldwell changed the name they were using from HomeSight to HomeTour, hoping to utilize the system's ability to show multiple pictures of a single property sequentially. Another set of changes involved personnel, both at Coldwell in Tampa and at DECOY. The test lost its local champion at Coldwell.

But perhaps most damaging for the test was a series of actions by the two parties that was fully revealed only after the test was complete. It began with AJH's unwillingness to charge adequately. There was a $25 per listing charge with a minimum monthly amount to be billed and a guarantee from Coldwell that "all listings" would be put on the system. In practice, only the minimum fee was charged, and HomeTour never had all of the listings. AJH was unwilling to press Coldwell for more because of the potential of the national rollout. An additional factor was the unwillingness of Coldwell to let DECOY personnel sell the system to the agents and teach them the benefits of using HomeTour. As it transpired,

Coldwell did an inadequate job of training and selling their agents; therefore, the agents did not perceive HomeTour as anything but an expensive substitute for newspaper advertising. Another problem arose from a change at Coldwell headquarters in what quantitative measures were to be used to determine success. Originally it was to be inquires; that was changed to "leads"; then to "sales generated by HomeTour." Thus a system that was designed to stop traffic–and thus generate inquiries–was measured against a goal–sales–that it was never intended to accomplish.

These changes were not communicated to DECOY until after the test was over. Despite all the difficulties and expense to DECOY to make changes that were never contemplated when the contract was negotiated–and which AJH never billed for–the test was a success by its original criteria. HomeSight *did* stop traffic. People *did* use the system. Sears executives were interested in what was going on, even though the machine planned for the Sears Tower in Chicago was never installed. HomeSight again proved itself a success at what it was designed to do.

In July 1987, executives from Coldwell and DECOY met in Newport Beach to discuss the future of HomeSight. In a two-hour meeting, it became clear that Coldwell was unwilling to continue with a national rollout at a price which would make profit for DECOY possible. In fact, it became clear at that meeting that Coldwell was not really interested in a rollout, regardless of price. Shortly after returning home, the Chairman killed HomeSight to pursue other projects.

At this point the saga of HomeSight, now named InfoVision, threatens to become a farce. Neither AJH nor the Chairman was willing to consider that Coldwell's unwillingness to go on to a national rollout might be the result of a product that, despite its promise, would join the innumerable caravan of products and services for which there is no market. The next two years were spent chasing after anyone who would evince any interest in the concept, spending time and other resources that could have been applied elsewhere around DECOY to better effect.

The first of these efforts was to install an InfoVision system, with listings for Cleveland, Ohio, at the Cleveland Home and Flower Show in early 1988. Again, traffic was stopped; several hundred ordinary people used the system and seemed generally delighted with it. However, the real estate agents and the owners of the two largest firms in Cleveland seemed totally uninterested. The project was killed for a second time.

The second effort, one which seemed at one time to have promise, was the installation of InfoVision at a mall near a mid-sized Ohio city; this effort started in mid-1988. It is a small enclosed mall set in an exurban market. Neither the store mix nor the people who shopped there seemed a priori to be potential heavy users of InfoVision. So why was it chosen? There were primarily two reasons. First, the Chairman would not let go; he constantly reiterated, "I've got X thousand dollars invested in this" when faced with the question of the future of InfoVision. Second, DECOY had had a long-standing relationship with this mall through one of its newspapers; the DECOY personnel–from the Chairman on down–knew the mall management and sold management on the idea. Unfortunately, the mall was not locally owned and getting corporate approval of the kiosk design became a process involving several months and many design changes.

In the meantime, InfoVision had undergone changes itself–not in the program or hardware, but in the concept of what InfoVision was to be. It had expanded into what was to be called "The InfoStore"– a manned, six-machine kiosk with listings for real estate, used and new cars, help wanted, medical referrals, and more. Much time and energy was devoted to making the referral system work, with talk about putting in audiotex or voice messaging to doctors, dentists, and realtors in order to prove that the InfoStore was providing customers. There was even discussion about holding "silent auctions" of certain types of merchandise on the system in order to get people to return and use the InfoStore. None of these ideas came to fruition–in fact, no software programming was started, nor was any hardware design–as the summer of 1988 wore on and DECOY still awaited approval of its InfoStore design from the mall owner.

Ultimately, the mall project collapsed primarily of its own weight. After spending additional thousands of dollars on kiosk designs, DECOY awoke to the fact that the kiosk would have to be manned 72 hours per week and would require at least two full-time employees to do so. The break-even point was raised geometrically with the added personnel cost, the use of six machines in one location, and the other system changes contemplated–and DECOY still had no idea who would pay, nor how much. What was worse, the more DECOY investigated the demographics and psychographics of the mall's market area in terms of InfoVision instead of the weekly newspaper it published, the more depressing the probabilities of success became. And this was to be another test, albeit one–it was fervently hoped–without financial risk to DECOY. After several months of work on the project, it was ultimately scrapped as unworkable, and InfoVision was killed yet a third time.

Last came the "grasping at straws" phase, resulting from the Chairman's insistence on using now-obsolete equipment because of sunk cost. An attempt was made to sell the hardware and its attendant software to a group of publishers of small real estate magazines in the South. These publishers wanted to put the machines in airports and malls, and use InfoVision as an adjunct to their magazines, not to generate revenue. The publishers offered no cash, and the purchase offer failed as a result.

Next, DECOY decided to use the machines to protect one of its most profitable *Homes Illustrated* markets. It contemplated placing all the listings from *Homes Illustrated* on the machine at no cost to keep a potential publishing competitor out. This attempt failed when DECOY could not obtain permission from mall owners for the kiosks. A similar approach to a grocery chain in Cleveland was also rebuffed.

Finally, in a last effort to find either money for further development or interest in taking the concept to the next plateau, DECOY took a booth at TechOhio. TechOhio is a conference and exhibition for new technological products and firms put on by Enterprise Development, Inc., an adjunct of Case Western Reserve University. There, DECOY made a separate, formal presentation to those in attendance. Although several other exhibitors came by the booth and seemed interested in the technology–particularly the touch-screen–no venture capitalist showed interest, nor did anyone else show any substantial interest in taking InfoVision to the next level. Nor, in fact, in taking the system as it stood and helping DECOY to market it. InfoVision died for the fourth time in June 1989. It may not be for the last time, however, as DECOY has a long-established pattern of resurrecting projects that have been given up as dead by everyone.

WHAT WENT WRONG?

A flippant answer would be "everything," but I do not think that everything went wrong. Many things were done right; it was simply that so many of the wrong things were done, or right things were not done that in retrospect InfoVision may have been doomed almost from its inception. I believe that the failure of InfoVision resulted from four different problems: cost, lack of proper organization, inability to terminate the project (discussed in detail in Part III, and only touched on here), and lack of marketing focus. These are not listed in order of importance, as there is no clear order of importance. In fact, all of these problems may be interwoven.

Cost

At the beginning, it was determined that InfoVision was to be presented to a probably computerphobic public as something other than a computer. This was the genesis of the touchscreen as the user input device, despite its cost of $1,500. On a machine that was delivered to a mall floor for $10,000, including its software and all hardware, that touchscreen represented too substantial a percentage of the total. Other hardware and kiosk design decisions combined to keep fixed costs relatively high, contributing to a price to the realtor of $25 per listing–and at that price DECOY was not making a large gross margin. Yet $25 per listing was higher than real estate agents were comfortable with; no research had gone into pricing the service prior to design of the system. Despite problems with hardware costs–as InfoVision continued through 1988 and 1989, with the obsolescence of much of the original hardware design–there was an adamant refusal on the part of both AJH and the Chairman to change one iota of the design. AJH was comfortable with the design decisions he had made in 1985, and the Chairman refused to consider scrapping any of his sunk costs. This refusal to change the hardware forced costs to remain high although alternatives for delivering equivalent or better performance had been developed since 1985 at lower cost, but would not be considered.

Lack of Organization

As mentioned previously, the usual DECOY practice for a new product idea or a new area for a publication was to give the person with the idea potential ownership in a company of which the Chairman owned all, with the idea person "sweating in" earnings until he and the Chairman each owned 50 percent. DECOY had been very successful through the years with this procedure. However, InfoVision was to expose the potential dangers inherent in this practice. First, AJH was introduced by the Chairman to outsiders as a "partner" when there was no agreement on management of the company nor who was to do what. In fact, leaving AJH in day-to-day control of the operation was a source of difficulty from the first. It was difficult for DECOY to find out what was going on, what bills were to be paid, what equipment had been purchased, and so on. In fact, during the Tampa test market, AJH hired employees to perform certain tasks without having them fill out employment applications, nor tax withholding forms, exposing DECOY to potential tax liability with both Internal Revenue and the state of Florida–where DECOY had no other operations and knew nothing about local tax law.

Over the period of operations, this lack of clarity in management and control eroded the relationship between the two individuals. Lack of trust in both directions grew deeper and deeper; in fact, the distrust of AJH permeated DECOY, hampering his effectiveness. Just before the third death of InfoVision, in July and August 1988, the two made one last attempt to work out their difficulties. Since AJH perceived himself to be in control of the operation even though he had no money invested–which conflicted with one of the Chairman's canons of business–this attempt was hopeless from the beginning. After the difficulties with InfoVision, coupled with another operation's all but failing from the same causes, the Chairman decided that his usual practice would have to be changed: no more 50 percent deals.

"Knee Deep in the Big Muddy"

The inability to stop development on the project turned a potentially small loss into a major financial and time drain on DECOY. Investment managers have a rule of thumb that one's first loss should be one's biggest loss, meaning that when losses start, one should sell out and try something else. A pithier way of saying this is "Starve the losers and feed the winners"–eminently good advice, but one much too often honored in the breach and not in the following.

No Marketing Focus

This section comprises three difficulties: no stability in service name, no clear fit with the rest of DECOY, and no clear concept of what the project was.

Although neither hardware nor software changed much from inception to the end of the project, the system used three names during its four-year life: VideoData, HomeSight, and InfoVision. This does not include HomeTour which was imposed by Coldwell Banker during the Tampa test. This lack of name stability would have confused users if there had been any; it certainly confused DECOY personnel.

Worse yet was the fact that the project had no clear fit with the rest of DECOY. Although eventually it was decided to try to sell InfoVision as a piggy-back product with *Homes Illustrated* in a major DECOY market, the system was originally contemplated as a stand-alone service. Although it utilized the *CompuAd* adwriting program, it was not seen as an adjunct to that family of products. Although the company should have been in the Electronic Publishing Division after DECOY's contemplated reorganization, the lack of a clear relationship with AJH would have made that unworkable. In short, InfoVision was a corporate orphan.

Worst of all, however, was the fact that no one had a clear concept of what the project was. Not until after the system had been assembled and placed into test market was anyone in the real estate business really asked whether the service made any sense, and there was never any formal market research undertaken. InfoVision does seem to fit the wants and needs of much of the real estate market, as discussed above, but much of this fit may be *post facto* justification.

Never during the development of InfoVision was the Marketing Concept so much as mentioned. Although the literature on new-service development is sparse, analogies to new-product development, with its burgeoning literature, can be followed. The lack of consideration for the marketing concept and lack of needs research into the market flies in the face of the work of Scheuing and Johnson (1987), von Hippel (1986), and Voss (1985a, 1985b).

Finally, the lessons of the test markets were ignored in the further marketing of InfoVision. It became apparent by the end of the Tampa test that InfoVision would only work as an adjunct to an existing publication, yet continuing efforts were made to make InfoVision a stand-alone system. And the Chairman vacillated as to whether DECOY should fund the continuing development or find a partner. Although there were advantages and disadvantages either way, one way or the other should have been pursued.

Although virtually everyone who ever saw InfoVision in operation was at least fascinated with the possibilities inherent in the new service, DECOY could never break through the problems mentioned above. It was not for lack of effort or resources; both of these were made available to InfoVision in abundance. Nevertheless, InfoVision failed. It is possible that it failed because of a lack of consistency in vision between the two principals; their dreams for the system were different from beginning to end, and there was no serious attempt to ever work out those differences in vision. However, it is equally likely that it failed because there is no real market for such a system, no matter how much a developer thinks there should be. The lack of any market research prior to its inception–or in fact, at any time during its life–makes this statement a conjecture, but one which I have been willing to make–indeed, have been making to the Chairman and in public–for several years.

PART III.
CONCLUSIONS AND IMPLICATIONS

Chapter 9

A Pause to Consider

Where are we now? We have discussed the tools of the Marketing Concept and perceptual mapping to determine what potential customers want and where gaps might be in the services already offered in a market. Three major cases have shown what can happen in the absence of those tools. What next?

Before proceeding to a discussion of what can be done beyond the use of the Marketing Concept and perceptual mapping, which in and of themselves do not solve the problem of how to successfully squeeze a new service into a crowded market, I would like to mention two additional sources of ambiguity in new services: the whole problem of escalation of effort, which is thoroughly discussed in Chapter 10, and innovation, which is discussed in Chapter 11.

Escalation of effort, a strand of research started by two management researchers, offers much food for thought in product and service introduction. My first exposure to the concept was in a *Harvard Business Review* article aptly entitled "Knowing When to Pull the Plug" (Staw and Ross, 1987b). The citations led me to the rest of the material cited in Chapter 10, including the even more perceptively named "Knee Deep in the Big Muddy" (Staw, 1976), which I have always thought of as the famous cartoon that has circulated in the office grapevine for years as the man standing in deep swamp water with the caption "When You're up to Your Ass in Alligators, It's Hard to Remember You Originally Went in to Drain the Swamp." All three of the cases in Part II are prime examples of difficulties with escalation of commitment. There is a fine line to be drawn between necessary perseverance and carrying on beyond all rational hope. The material presented in Chapter 10 should help the reader to understand where to draw that line.

Innovation–that greatly sought goal of all organizations in the 1990s–is problematical at best. We are all exhorted in the popular business press to be innovative. Academic business scholars have pursued research for at least a decade showing that innovation is necessary and continuous innovation is even better than sporadic innovation; and yet, innovation by definition means doing new things or doing old things in a new way. Engineers and management scholars may be forgiven for thinking that innovation is great; marketers may need to have second thoughts: what if the customers do not wish for anything new? What if they are happy with what they have? Does too much innovation merely confuse them? Confused customers are not likely to be happy customers. I have written on this topic before; nothing in the years since the first piece was written has caused me to be less emphatic about this point. Quite the reverse. My on-going observation of the computer hardware and software business convinces me more than ever that too many innovations occur because they *can* be done, not because anyone outside the organization doing the innovating wants them to be done.

Chapter 10

Escalation of Commitment

What do we mean by "escalation of commitment"? Simply put it is the persistence of movement in the face of indications that persistence should be stopped, that the movement is proceeding in the wrong direction or has gone too far, that good money is now being thrown after bad. The research in this area has primarily been done by Jerry Ross and Barry Staw, and reported in Staw (1976), Staw and Ross (1987a, 1987b), and Ross and Staw (1993). The latter article reports on the case of the Shoreham nuclear power plant, built by Long Island Lighting Company (LILCO) at the cost of $5.1 billion, but never put into service. It is the perfect exemplar of escalation of commitment, as it was originally projected to cost around $70 million and take three years to build; by the end, it never generated electricity, cost $5.1 billion, almost bankrupted LILCO, and resulted in a long round of intense political negotiations among several levels of government to determine what was to be done. According to Ross and Staw (1993), the indicators of escalation, which they call "escalation determinants," fall into three categories.

PROJECT DETERMINANTS

The dynamics of a project itself, whether the *Edition* or InfoVision, truly appear to be minimal in a real situation. Rather, the category more clearly can be viewed as individual or organizational failure to recognize reality than any anthropomorphosis of "The Project." Ross and Staw (1993) cite a great deal of literature on managements' coping with sunk costs–probably the classic "project determinant" without ever stating that the failure to deal with such costs as "money poured down a hole" is *psychological*. At one point in the life of the *Edition,* I was invited in by Gunlocke to prepare an offer to buy the paper on behalf of one of my clients. Gunlocke's accountant scoffed at my client's offer because Gunlocke had "more than that invested" in the property. The subsequent demise of the paper showed that none of that money was truly invested, as I said at the time; it was all sunk.

CONTEXTUAL DETERMINANTS

In the Ross and Staw (1993) example these determinants occurred because Shoreham became big enough to threaten LILCO's ability to survive or provide electricity to Long Island. An organization of this size warrants intervention by outsiders. None of the cases described in Part II was this large and, therefore, there were no contextual determinants. However, if the organization which has escalated its commitment is large enough to have major impact on a community or larger entity, it is apt to be bailed out of its management's stupidity by the body politic. Another clear case of this happening is the Chrysler bailout by the Federal Government in the early 1980s.

PSYCHOLOGICAL, SOCIAL, AND ORGANIZATIONAL DETERMINANTS

Given the facts that both DECOY and the *Edition* were wholly owned by one man, InfoVision as a company was, at best, a two-man partnership; and the corporate staff of DECOY was minuscule. All of these determinants are totally interwoven and inextricably bound up in one. As entrepreneurial firms with strong owners, willing to allow a lot of operational freedom to achieve the owners' goals, both DECOY and the *Edition* were essentially the owner writ large. His psychological profile was the firm's psychological profile. The Chairman used his success in business psychologically, continuing a constant string of successes begun in childhood.

When InfoVision, Triples, and the Colorado *Homes Illustrated* operation simultaneously soured, along with the first indications of other difficulties within DECOY, Inc., it unnerved him. He had no history of failing at anything, so he had no idea of how to deal with it. As a result he pressed on in all of these endeavors, throwing good money after bad. Relentlessly. Against all advice. As did Bill Gunlocke with the *Edition*; the paper continually reappeared every time Gunlocke got a few nickles in his jeans, with almost no changes. The readers were happy and that was all he seemed to care about.

EXIT BECAME PSYCHOLOGICALLY IMPOSSIBLE

The fact that there were no "divisions" in the Empire, that anyone could be thrown into any project at any time, that the corporate staff was so small, had the salubrious effect of giving a very broad background to the team. However, it also made it impossible for anyone but the Chairman to collate what was going on, which made it very easy for his relentless pursuit of success in the face of internal opposition and external realities. When Coldwell Banker decided that $25 per listing was too much to pay for a national InfoVision program, it was impossible for DECOY to regroup, meet with people from Coldwell to ascertain what they would pay, and how both the equipment and payment could be restructured, because the necessary people were off working on other projects, and there were no spare bodies to put into the gaps. Gunlocke flew the *Edition* by the seat of his pants. When potential investors presented themselves at his door, they were foisted off onto his extremely uncooperative accountant, who somehow seemed not to realize the seriousness of the problems at the *Edition,* nor how to evaluate the firm to present it to potential buyers.

This is hardly an exhaustive discussion of these determinants, nor is it meant to be. It simply points out two difficulties that entrepreneurs of family-run businesses seem to have that are endemic and internal. First, their reaction to their previous work experiences; second, their desire to pass their firms (or their value) to their heirs.

The Chairman of DECOY had not worked long for others before starting his own family business in his early 30s. However, his employment experiences were basically negative and somewhat traumatic. So traumatic, in fact, that 30 years later one heard about them when suggestions were made that sounded too much like the way things had been done during previous employment. Further, he was very much a "people" person. Not only did he talk on the telephone daily to a large network of friends, colleagues, associates, and employees in order to obtain information, but most of his partners were also friends of long standing. One was a college roommate; another knew him since boyhood. It was extremely difficult for staff or consultants to discuss drastic measures under these circumstances. Although the "partner" who dreamed up InfoVision was *not* a friend, he arrogated the partner status ("partners don't have to give the Chairman bad news–that's what employees are there for") with a vengeance.

Although cronyism certainly is not the sole preserve of the entrepreneur, it is probably more common in an entrepreneurial company, particularly a small- to medium-size one. And its impact is certainly more devastating than in large firms which can swaddle upper management with staffs and middle managers whose jobs are to run the organization despite interference or incompetence above. At DECOY there was no staff to speak of and no middle managers to protect the firm from senior management. Gunlocke clearly reacted to his past history as the heir to a family-owned and operated business; he saw what it had done to his father and, like many children of the 1960s, he did not like it and did not want to repeat the experience in his life. He viewed himself as the English teacher he had once been and would be again, even while he was publishing a newspaper with several employees who needed to be dealt with as employees instead of as students.

Equally problematical is the desire of owners of family-owned businesses to pass on value to their heirs–a desire, of course, no different from others, but in the case of a family-owned business, often the firm represents an enormous percentage of the assets of the family. This fact, when added to the fact that often a large percentage of the family's income is also derived from the firm (also the case with both DECOY and the Chairman's family, and the *Edition*–although not Gunlocke's family), and the psychological importance of preserving the firm no matter what becomes clear.

The Chairman was one of the founders of the National Association of Real Estate Publishers, a group of entrepreneurial-like spirits in the *Homes* magazine industry. One of the publishers had developed a laser-disc version of a *Homes* magazine, photographing every house on Hilton Head Island. Others were interested in the implications of *CompuAd*. All were well aware of the fact that their black-and-white, newsprint magazines were obsolescent if not obsolete in the face of television, a generation raised on color media, and the fact that people were spending more and more time at the mall–InfoVision's expected site. If the Chairman were to preserve value in DECOY for his heirs, if he were to continue long-term, something had to be added to *Homes Illustrated*, and *CompuAd* never sold well enough to give much hope that it would be the core business for the new century. InfoVision could be that core business and, because of his need for value and the social determinant of technologically progressive colleagues in an industry association, InfoVision was born. Gunlocke operated in a different sphere entirely, but clearly had some aspirations to be able to meet as a peer with his colleagues in the alternative-press world.

Finally Ross and Staw dig into the real problem with escalation which is stasis–what they call the "permanently failing organization" (1993: 725, after Meyer and Zucker, 1989). InfoVision–at least after the failure to successfully negotiate a next stage with Coldwell–and *Locus* were permanently failing projects; but DECOY has a history of permanently failing projects that are never allowed to die. The *Edition* also fits neatly into this category. Ross and Staw (1993) developed 12 propositions with regard to escalation of commitment (see Table 10.1). I have modified six of them for entrepreneurial enterprises, and will introduce and discuss them below. The numbers in parentheses refer to the original Ross and Staw proposition numbers.

Proposition A (8): When internal stakeholders are strong enough to continue a losing project or service, it will create a permanently failing operation. The propensity for this is especially strong in entrepreneurial enterprises and/or where the developer of the project is very senior in an organization.

CompuAd, now in its fifth generation with one or more major rewrites in development, is another case in point at DECOY. Here the

TABLE 10.1. Escalation Propositions

Proposition 1: Organizational escalation is determined by a combination of psychological, project, social, and organizational determinants.

Proposition 2: There is a temporal ordering in the influence of the determinants of organizational escalation—project variables are most important at the early stages of an escalation episode, psychological and social variables are dominant at the middle stages, and both organizational and project considerations become most influential at the late or ending stage of the typical escalation episode.

Proposition 3: The earlier organizational determinants occur in an escalation episode, the more likely there will be long-term commitment to a course of action.

Proposition 4: The more external political forces become aligned with a project, the more difficult it will be for the initiating organization to withdraw from the course of action.

Proposition 5: The more ambiguous and changing the economics of a project, the more difficult it will be for an organization to extricate itself from the selected course of action.

Proposition 6: When the potential losses of a project become so large that withdrawal might lead to bankruptcy, an organization becomes increasingly committed to the losing endeavor.

Proposition E: When termination of a project will prevent an entrepreneur from increasing the asset value of the firm, project termination will be difficult.

Proposition 7: Escalation problems are especially likely to occur when managers venture far from their areas of expertise or when technological changes cause such major changes in an organizational context that previously learned procedures and decision checks are no longer applicable.

Proposition D: Innovation only causes escalation problems when the project does not come in on time and on budget. The more experience a firm or an entrepreneur has with successful innovation, even innovation unrelated to the current project, the more likely it will be that escalation/exit difficulties will occur when a project is delayed or has cost overruns.

Proposition 8: When external constituents are successful in preventing the closing of a losing project or service, the unsuccessful firm or department may become a permanently failing organization.

Proposition A: When internal stakeholders are strong enough to continue a losing project or service, it will create a permanently failing operation. The propensity for this is especially strong in entrepreneurial enterprises and/ or where the developer of the project is very senior in an organization.

Proposition 9: Changes in top management can reduce psychological and social sources of commitment, thus increasing the propensity for withdrawal from a losing course of action.

Proposition 10: Efforts to deinstitutionalize a project, or to separate it from the central goals and purposes of an enterprise, can reduce organizational determinants of commitment, thereby increasing the propensity for withdrawal.

Proposition B: Efforts to deinstitutionalize a project in an entrepreneurial company when initiated by those other than the entrepreneur or shareholders will probably cause the entrepreneur to proceed more forcefully with the losing project.

Proposition 11: Appeals to favoring organizational constituencies (for new loans and support) can change a project's economics so that withdrawal is not so costly and thus more likely to be chosen as an alternative.

Proposition C: Changing the reality of a project's economics in an entrepreneurial firm will mean little without changing the psychology of the project for the entrepreneur.

Proposition 12: Threats to persevere in a losing course of action can influence opposing constituencies to change a project's economics, thus making it less costly (and more likely) for withdrawal to occur.

Proposition F: Once hard costs have been spent, and the easier it is to hide soft costs (even from oneself), the less incentive the organization will have to terminate a project. Conversely, if hard costs continue to run, the organization will be forced on a regular basis to confront the "terminate or continue" issue.

Numbered propositions from Ross & Staw (1993); lettered propositions are those derived from the research presented here.

idea was the Chairman's; no lack of sales success with this product will ever kill it so long as he is alive.

Proposition B (10): Efforts to deinstitutionalize a project in an entrepreneurial company when initiated by those other than the entrepreneur or shareholders will probably cause the entrepreneur to proceed more forcefully with the losing project.

Examples of Proposition B are legion in the recent past. The only way that this dilemma seems to be resolved is if the outsiders–be they employees, lenders, or whomever–can get enough leverage to force the entrepreneur to the sidelines and salvage the firm–often at the expense of the losing project. Steve Jobs at Apple Computer and Edwin Land at Polaroid are classic examples. Likewise

Proposition C (11): Changing the reality of a project's economics in an entrepreneurial firm will mean little without changing the psychology of the project for the entrepreneur.

But it is Ross and Staw's Proposition 7 (1993:724) that needs the most restatement for entrepreneurial firms, for so many of them venture far afield of the entrepreneur's background almost by definition. New *firms* have no organization history or experience; founders of those firms tend to have unbalanced experience. The Chairman left being a small-town-newspaper reporter originally to start a printing business; Gunlocke had been a schoolteacher and a bookstore owner/manager. In a sense, the history of successful entrepreneurial ventures is a history of escalation. Thus

Proposition D (7): Innovation only causes escalation problems when the project does not come in on time and on budget. The more experience a firm or an entrepreneur has with successful innovation, even innovation unrelated to the current project, the more likely it will be that escalation/exit difficulties will occur when a project is delayed or has cost overruns.

Ronstadt (1988) discusses the importance to entrepreneurs' careers of venturing afield from even their entrepreneurial experience. As business success piles upon earlier personal success, the entrepreneur's ability to "pull the plug" quickly diminishes.

INNOVATION AND ESCALATION
IN THE ENTREPRENEURIAL/FAMILY-OWNED FIRM

An entrepreneur who has a firm in a mature industry–such as the Chairman of DECOY, firmly ensconced in two disparate aspects of black-and-white newsprint publishing–can feel the hot breath of obsolescence and declining value upon a firm he or she is trying to pass on to the next generation. Therefore, the entrepreneur is faced with a problem of how to increase, or at least stabilize, the value of the firm. One way is to make an acquisition or series of acquisitions; however, if the entrepreneur is afraid of building a bureaucracy, this is probably not a viable option. Another way is to sell the firm; however, if family members are working in the firm, this option may also not be viable.

Therefore, diversification by innovation may be particularly appealing to the entrepreneur. Thus

> *Proposition E (6): When termination of a project will prevent an entrepreneur from increasing the asset value of the firm, project termination will be difficult.*

InfoVision is a clear case in point. The Chairman clearly hoped that InfoVision coupled with *CompuAd* would take DECOY into the next century with an interactive color real estate medium that would appeal more than the static black-and-white newsprint *Homes Illustrated* books; this was also true of *Locus,* although to a lesser extent. Although neither InfoVision nor *Locus* was a "bet the company" project, InfoVision was clearly an attempt by the Chairman to emulate Ted Williams and hit a home run in his last at bat. So long as he did not publicly terminate the project, hope could continue. And yet it is apparent that the Chairman knew that InfoVision was hopeless after the last meeting with Coldwell in Newport Beach; no further money was spent on equipment or software development. Money *was* spent, but it was spent on attempts to get another test market or on maintenance of hardware or software, anything to keep InfoVision alive and out in the public eye. Not one penny went to improve performance or deal with any of the changes which users had mentioned during the test markets or at trade shows. Clearly the technology expenditures were a classic example of sunk costs hanging about the Chairman's neck like an albatross.

> *Proposition F: Once hard costs have been spent, and the easier it is to hide soft costs (even from oneself), the less incentive the organization will have to terminate a project. Conversely,*

> *if hard costs continue to run, the organization will be forced on a regular basis to confront the "terminate or continue" issue.*

The Chairman as a young newspaper publisher was quite ruthless in closing newspapers; as he said of one of his partners: "Two losing weeks in a row and POW! the [guy] would shut down and move on." Although there are other causes of this effect–the Chairman was younger, the financial impact of any of these small weekly papers was much less than InfoVision's, a partner was making the actual decisions and the Chairman only ratifying them–a major cause was the weekly print-run figure and the monthly income statement. As the Chairman was dealing with InfoVision, he was also wrestling with *Locus*. Although closing *Locus* was also painfully slow, it ultimately was only the fact that a weekly print run and monthly income statement were prepared showing actual cash losses each month which allowed the Chairman to terminate *Locus*. Once InfoVision had gone through the Tampa test market, the cash outflow each month was small; there was no burning necessity to publicly terminate it. As the project slipped farther in time from the test market, the smaller the cash outflow became, further reducing the incentive.

The research effort evidenced by Ross and Staw (1993) and their previous articles is vitally important, nowhere more so than for entrepreneurial and family-owned enterprises. Although a Shoreham nuclear facility–a $5 billion plant–is enormously dramatic, the losses from an InfoVision or an *Edition* can be just as devastating to the entrepreneur. Shoreham's loss was spread to all of LILCO's shareholders and rate payers and, ultimately, to the taxpayers of New York State. InfoVision's loss was borne by one man and his family, as was the *Edition's*. *Locus's* loss was spread to three owners and their families.

Entrepreneurs are not uniquely vulnerable to escalation of commitment; the Shoreham experience proves that fact. For-profit businesses do not even have a monopoly on escalation; Expo '86 (Ross and Staw, 1986) shows evidence proving that fact. *Projects* are subject to escalation of commitment. Projects have project managers and project-team members, whose jobs are threatened if and when the project is terminated; thus the personnel involved have incentives to keep the projects going, no matter what.

What can management attempting to squeeze new services into crowded markets do in the face of these facts? This question is important particularly since new products and services seem to be especially vulnerable to underestimation of difficulties at the start. This led to the desire to persist in the face of difficulties since everyone will know that the difficulties were underestimated and "just one more push" may make the difference.

As hard as it may be to do, managements *must* set realistic budgets of time and resources which are available and will not be overspent in the face of difficulties before embarking on a new venture. Although AJH sent me a mug labelled "Budgets are for Wimps" when I started putting budgets into place for another attempt at getting InfoVision to succeed (in 1987), budgets are an absolute necessity. When the budgeted resources or time are exhausted, an opportunity has presented itself for a meaningful review of the situation. Is it true that "one more push" will bring things off? Or are we merely throwing good money after bad? It becomes a clear-cut opportunity to starve the losers and use those resources to feed potential winners.

This review must be rigidly and rigorously rational and free from wishful thinking. It must not be an occasion where the product champion, through superior rhetorical skill, can overwhelm experience and the numbers. The perceptual maps must be brought out again and restudied, along with any other research that has been done. And the data probably should be analyzed by a dispassionate, outside, third party who has no axe to grind. When the champion is the Chairman of the firm, such a rational analysis is difficult; if the champion is the Chairman of an entrepreneurial firm who is looking for a home run, such a rational analysis is probably impossible.

Chapter 11

Innovation

There is a story, unfortunately probably apocryphal, about a county extension agent–fresh out of the state agricultural college–who was driving a back road quite a ways from anywhere. He saw an old farmer using antiquated techniques and equipment, of the type that his professors had railed against repeatedly, holding up this type of farmer as an exemplar of the very person whom the extension agent should try to reform. Well, the extension agent got out of his car and tried to reform this old farmer. Finally, the old man had had enough. He took his hat off, spit tobacco juice in the general direction of the young man's shoes, scratched himself in several places, and said, "Tell you what, sonny; everything you say might be right. Probably is, what with you've been to college and all. But, hell, boy, I already don't farm near as good as I know how."

The extent to which American farmers have changed in their approach to innovations and have, in fact, become innovators of farming implements and techniques, creating new firms, patenting their inventions, and successfully marketing some of them, is clearly spelled out in Carlson (1993). Further, innovative successes in marketing their output at retail, either in the form of specialty produce or branded processed foods–such as mustard–often at quite high prices, have also come to some who have tried; witness the $18.95 delivered price for a "baker's dozen" of Idaho potatoes! (*Marketing News,* 1994).

I do not cite the old-farmer story as an example of why we should all be open to innovation; rather, it is a plea to be careful of innovating, lest we leave behind not only those who do not understand the innovations, but also the people–and thus markets–for whom the innovation is meaningless since they reached a plateau which met their needs a few innovations earlier.

Everett Rogers, probably the leading authority on innovation, defines an innovation as an

> idea, practice, or object that is perceived as new by an individual or another unit of adoption. An innovation presents an individual or an organization with a new alternative or alternatives, with new means of solving problems. (Rogers, 1983: xviii-xix)

But the probabilities of the innovation's superiority to the old way are not known, so the individuals must seek information on the innovation in order to cope with its uncertainty; there will be more about this information-seeking in a later section of this chapter. The *Webster's New World Dictionary* has a simpler, more concise, definition: "something newly introduced; new method, custom, device, etc.; change in the way of doing things." Robertson and Gatignon (1987) discuss how supply-side factors influence the diffusion of technological innovations, as well as how competition influences the adopters in their use of the innovations.

Still innovation, although it is inextricably linked with creativity, is not the same thing as creativity. Creativity is the process of identifying either a problem that was previously unrecognized or a solution that is novel or outside the experience of others (Edwards and Sproull, 1984). According to Dauw (1969:85), innovation is an organizational or social process that follows invention–"the product of an original, elaborating, highly creative thinker who can usually germinate novel ideas rather fluently"–which is highly personal.

There are many opportunities for, or constraints upon the process; however, they may be categorized into two overarching groupings: environmental and internal to the firm (United States Department of Commerce, 1983:67-68). Environmental factors consist of:

- The technological base
- Overall economic conditions
- Price stability
- Industry composition
- Government policies
- Research and Development incentives

The state of overall knowledge in the economy can be a severe constraint. Not only is it difficult to innovate if the necessary technological support is not present, but if the proper infrastructure does not exist, it may be impossible. How many inventions have been labelled "before their time" simply because some small ancillary system did not exist? Mark Twain's *A Connecticut Yankee in King Arthur's Court* is a marvelous example. Although Eli Whitney's introduction of assembling rather complicated machinery from interchangeable parts occurred almost 200 years ago, the standards of precision in machining tools at the time precluded close tolerances limiting the applicability of the innovation.

Equally important is the state of knowledge of customers and potential customers. If the firm must spend a lot of time educating customers on the purpose of a new product–what I call "Missionary Selling"–resources become diverted from other parts of the marketing mix and the entire marketing effort may bog down. Although there is extensive literature on the profits to be gained by being a pioneer in a market (for reviews of this literature, see Aaker and Day, 1986; Alpert, 1987), it is often easier for a firm to enter a market that someone else has started (and educated to the benefits of the generic category)–as IBM did with personal computers. Failing entering someone else's market, management probably will at least breathe easier when competition arrives on the scene and legitimates the market, even if the competition does cut into one's market share somewhat.

Overall economic conditions place severe constraints on introductions of innovative products and services when conditions are negative–although recessions may encourage the introduction of goods and services which promise to make firms more efficient. In contrast positive conditions provide various opportunities.

At least as important a consideration is price stability. Periods of high inflation and extreme financial-market volatility lead firms to favor short-term investments with relatively low risk; a firm trying to introduce an innovation which will take three or four years to show results, but will then show extraordinary returns to firms which adopt the innovation, will probably have difficulty successfully introducing the innovation under these conditions. However, if there is relatively little inflation and stable financial markets, firms will be more inclined to make long-term investments in projects with higher risks. They do this if for no other reason than the returns to which they have become accustomed in financial instruments are absent and the annual price increase "to cover inflation" cannot be instituted because inflation is low and competitors may be willing to buy market share by not instituting a price increase.

Industry structure is also important as a constraint/opportunity. Innovations seem to be most common in industries characterized by the presence of many firms of relatively similar size. Economic theory would indicate that industries characterized as monopolies or oligopolies should see innovative behavior less often rarely than industries where the firms are engaged in freer competition. Although specific exceptions to theoretical expectations can be found, certainly the recent past would seem to indicate that theory matches empirical results.

Governmental policies in two areas have major roles in this discussion: antitrust guidelines, and those safeguards of intellectual property–trademarks, patents, copyrights, etc. In many respects these two are opposite poles on a continuum; to the extent that intellectual property safeguards are strong, they will lead in time to monopolistic control of a market. The history of federal government policies in this area seems to cycle between strong enforcement of one end of the continuum or the other. If intellectual property protections are strong, one should expect more innovative behavior; if antitrust enforcement is high, one might expect less.

The final environmental factor falls on the general incentives for research and development projects. These incentives have many faces: straight tax inducements for research and development such as the tax credits; governmental purchase programs such as military or National Aeronautical and Space Administration procurement; "seed" money or small research grants to start potential commercially viable projects on their way; venture capitalists who wish to invest early in possibly viable products; and many more. The presence of these kinds of incentives may help to spur the development of innovations; it is more likely that they enable innovations which have been proposed to make it to the first stages of commercial viability than to encourage creativity or innovation per se.

Factors internal to the corporation consist of:

- Corporate goals
- Corporate financial profile
- Managerial quality

Corporate goals setting the desired rate of return from projects, desired market share for products or services offered, desired rates of growth, etc., drive firm's day-to-day operational decisions about entertaining new products or services. For example, if desired rates of return are high, coupled with a short payback period, it could be difficult to justify many new projects.

The corporate financial profile can be crucial to the firm's ability to develop new products or services, place new plant and equipment into service, or seek to expand market share. If a firm has a high degree of debt acquired as a part of a leveraged buyout, that debt could conceivably hamper management's short-term ability to add new products or services (Fox and Marcus, 1992). If a firm has good positive cash flow, on the other hand, "buying" market share with new projects may be feasible.

Managerial quality, on the other hand, is more difficult to analyze objectively, especially from outside the firm. The level of management's understanding of the technological base of the industry, for example, may preclude a firm's entering into a long-term research and development project if management personnel have only recently come from a different industry with different technological needs. But vastly outweighing this management characteristic is management's overall comfort with risk. Innovation is, by definition, fraught with risk. Can a firm's management stand the heat? Can it adequately reward the people on whom it depends for developing the innovation without, on the one hand straining the firm's system of rewards and punishments, nor on the other hand turning the development "team" into disgruntled ex-employees who will immediately set up a competing firm?

Services are often described as having the unique characteristics of intangibility, inseparability or simultaneity, perishability, and heterogeneity or uneven quality of delivery. The impact that the presence of these characteristics has and should have upon innovation will be discussed below.

Intangibility–the lack of any concrete "product" or "outcome" to a service encounter–has a major impact upon service delivery at all levels and at all times. Intangibility is the driving force behind everything associated with services and services marketing. Although product marketers may have difficulties with the nontangible portion of their offerings, services marketers have nothing but the nontangible component. Therefore, customers take almost nothing away from a service encounter but the experience. There may be a will or a tax return–a small tangible component, even though neither the will nor the return is truly encompassed by the piece of paper in the client's hand (and even less so for an electronically filed return)–but the encounter is as evanescent as a play. It is this evanescence which has led to the work of Grove and Fisk (1992, 1989), Grove, Fisk, and Bitner (1992), and Grove, Fisk, and Kenny (1990) on the service encounter as theater.

Inseparability or simultaneity–the fact that services are usually "consumed" as they are "produced," and often in the presence of and with input from the customer–leads to considering services as drama as much as intangibility does. Furthermore, this "complicity"–and certainly the physical presence on the part of the customer–makes services marketers think about the impact of the physical premises upon the customer. It may be true that no one should watch sausage being made; this operation can be screened from the public. But one must meet with the lawyer doing one's will, or the accountant doing the tax return; one has information which must be imparted to those individuals in order for them to do their jobs properly. The stage must, therefore, be properly set in order to give the client the proper confidence that the operatives can perform their jobs satisfactorily.

Perishability–the fact that many services are time-dependant at creation and cannot be stockpiled into inventory–has a major impact on both pricing elasticities and supply pressures. Once the airplane takes off, any empty seats will never produce revenue on that flight; once the unbilled hour is over, it can never be recaptured. With this fact in mind, it becomes more readily apparent that many service firms face tremendous pressures to make it possible to utilize all of their providers at whatever price necessary to achieve this level of utilization. Unlike a traditional (manufacturing) analysis, many service firms–particularly professional service firms–have virtually no "fixed" costs other than salary and benefits; therefore, there is no need to ensure that someone pays the overhead before reducing price to cover the variable costs. Almost all costs are thus, in effect, costs per hour. Therefore it is better to be paid a fraction of the normal hourly rate than not be paid at all for an elapsed hour, for which employees need to be paid whether they earned revenue for the firm or not. I do not wish to push this line of reasoning too far; it is simply necessary here to recognize the fact of its existence.

Uneven quality or heterogeneity–the quality directly attributable to the fact that service providers are people and thus make mistakes–causes a great deal of concern for service providers. The considerations raised in general above apply with extraordinary force to professional-service firms who have nothing tangible to give to clients. An airplane trip may be intangible, but at least the passenger can sit in a tangible seat in a tangible airplane. A restaurant meal may be intangible, but at least the food is tangible, if not permanent. How tangible is a will? A financial consultation? A share of stock? There may be tangible *evidence* of these transactions–the "paper copy" of the will, a copy of the financial plan, a certificate representing the share of stock (but, perhaps, only a statement from the brokerage firm that the share is somewhere on deposit–unknown and undisclosed to the client, and in fact possibly rehypothecated to a bank by the brokerage firm).

Furthermore, in many professional-service experiences, demand for the service is not truly driven by the client; rather it is "environmentally driven." How many audited corporate financial statements would be produced in the absence of a requirement that all publicly held corporations present audited financial statements annually to their shareholders? How many times would individuals have their wills re-written in the absence of changes in the federal income and estate tax laws? How often would a consulting firm be able to sell its services to clients for ideas that *it* had for a client rather than responding to a request by a potential client that the firm help with the client's ideas?

What causes the failure of professional services for clients? In addition to the general characteristics of services mentioned above, there seem to be three specific characteristics of the services provided by professional firms that cause difficulty: professional services are often never "used" or are "single use" at best; professional services are often temporally separated widely between production and use; and the newness in service components repeatedly forced by environmental forces leads to uneven quality.

Professional services are often never used. I am currently on my third will; the first two were, obviously, not used. When the tax laws change substantially again, I suppose that I will have to go in for will number four; although this is clearly not the fault of my attorney, I am not happy to have to pay him to prepare a revision of my will that was caused by no change in my personal circumstances. And, of course, I have no idea how well written the will is; a will is the quintessential "single-use" item. If it is poorly drawn, there is no hope for improvement the next time, or what Berry and Parasuraman (1991) call "doing the service very right the second time." But wills are not the only "one-offs"; my consulting engagements are almost totally project based rather than on-going relationships. I only have one chance to give the correct advice. (For further examples, see Hart, Heskett, and Sasser, 1990).

The example of a will is a also good one to use for the wide temporal separation between the "production" of a service and its "use" that can occur with professional services. We are so conditioned by thinking of services as inseparable and intangible that we forget that the service produced–the will–is only part of the total service. Until the person for whom the will is drawn dies and the estate is probated under the terms of that will, *the service is not complete*. Three years may elapse between the time an accountant files a tax return for an individual or corporation and the Internal Revenue Service conducts a review or an audit; until that lapse of time, *the service is not complete*. This temporal separation of parts of the service raises the level of risk for the client, certainly in the client's perception.

Finally, newness of services leads to irregular or even bad quality in the service provided. It takes time for professionals to digest new laws or regulations or methods of solving client problems. During the time when this digestion is taking place, it is possible–indeed, even probable–that some clients will get advice or documents which are incorrect or certainly unclear. After the time necessary for reflection and internalizing changes has passed, uniformity in documents and advice will occur again. However, the transition period will be fraught with danger for the client–and, ultimately, for the provider as well, who will need to ascertain which clients have not been well served during the interregnum.

There are risks to users and providers alike caused by failure of the service, no matter what the cause of that failure. These risks fall into two major categories: reputation and financial. The risk to reputation because of a service failure can be at least as damaging as the direct financial impact–especially to the service provider, for whom the loss of reputation will probably lead to financial impact–for providers often have little to differentiate themselves from the competition and little to offer clients or potential clients save their reputation. A law firm which is fined by regulators for violating the canons of ethics or regulatory procedures will find it more difficult to convince prospects and customers that their work will be properly handled by the firm in the future. And the firm may find that existing clients become concerned enough about the potential for the client's reputation to be tainted by association with the firm, to find another firm to do their work. Likewise, if a client finds its name in the paper as subject to an audit or penalty from an audit because of improperly performed work on the part of its accounting firm, even if the client does not sue, a certain chill is likely to invade the relationship.

A client of mine had to file an amended tax return less than two weeks after the original return had been filed because of the failure of his accountant to include $250,000 in rental income on the client's personal return that the same accountant had deducted as rental expense on the client's corporate return. Then the accountant sent my client a bill for preparing and filing the amended return! In the end, of course, the accountant rescinded the bill. Needless to say, however, the relationship between my client and his accountant was soured and, although the client still retains this accounting firm, the relationship has never returned to its former warmth.

How do service firms get out of the box caused by the intersection of the characteristics of service firms and the desire for innovation? There seem to be three avenues out of the dilemma, not necessarily mutually exclusive. They are: the use of unconditional service guarantees, a reduction in innovation itself, and the use of an expert-system approach to the problem. Unconditional service guarantees are extensively discussed in Chapter 12. A second avenue out of the dilemma seems to be for the firm to simply reduce its striving for innovation. Although this avenue seems to fly in the face of advice, particularly from the practitioner arena, to "increase competitiveness through innovativeness," the drive for increased innovation has real problems for clients and providers alike, which have been mentioned above.

Perhaps simply reducing the number of new ideas which a firm will consider might help to stabilize the delivery of quality services to clients. Recall the story of the farmer and the extension agent which started this chapter; we may not be providing services "as good as we know how"–why try something new? If, for whatever reason, this approach seems to be inappropriate for a particular firm, perhaps reducing its innovativeness in exchange for finding new ways of *producing and delivering* the firm's existing services will achieve the same end. If demand for many services is environmental in nature, innovative *delivery systems* will allow firms to differentiate themselves from their competition *while providing essentially identical offerings* and lowering the risks of innovation to both the providers and their clients.

Innovation, however, has such a strong hold on the American consciousness, particularly the American business consciousness, that I doubt that many service providers will heed my warning about reducing the amount of innovation in the firm. This seems particularly relevant since the latest study on innovation (Jelinek and Schoonhoven, 1993) recommends a process of *continuous* innovation for firms to continue to be successful and able to compete with world-class firms in the future.

All of this emphasis on reducing innovation may sound strange in a book devoted to helping firms squeeze a *new* service into a crowded market. Nevertheless, I am including this chapter as a plea to slow down and investigate the options before plunging ahead. There are, after all, three ways of increasing revenue: selling more of the existing service(s) to existing customers, selling existing services to new customers, and selling new services. Only the latter is truly innovative, with all of its inherent difficulties for customers and the firm. The first is the domain of the sales literature, as it deals with more effective selling. The second, however, has great promise for most firms.

It is extremely unlikely that markets have been adequately tapped for the firm's existing service(s). Bank trust departments, for example, tend to have minimum fees based upon arbitrary desired account sizes which discourage people whose assets are smaller than that minimum from opening accounts, even if their accounts will be larger in a short period of time. Economically justified lower fees–with lower service/contact standards–can attract this marginal business, with the understanding that the account will move to regular service standards when the asset size so warrants. The firm which can find a way to penetrate otherwise ignored markets with existing or slightly modified methods of doing business can reap tremendous profit margins and make the customers very happy because they thought that they might not qualify for that kind of offering. The success of the legal-clinic concept in the 1980s has shown the way.

This type of innovation reduces the risk of "over-innovation" to the firm because it is generally offering the same, or nearly the same, service; it is simply the clientele that is different. Of course, the service providers will need to be sensitive to the differences of the new market, or they will have problems caused by expecting the old client segment's behavior from the new segment. But the providers will need little or no training on the new offering, reducing costs and chaos to the firm. And it is these costs that make innovating by selling new services so expensive.

Chapter 12

Unconditional Service Guarantees

For a service firm to be successful, it must consistently provide services which meet the expectations of its clients, just as a product firm must consistently produce products which meet the expectations of its customers. As we shall see, this matching requires a substantial amount of effort and organization. And, if the firm is unable to match expectation with performance, all its other marketing and management efforts–even the accurate performance of the *service* for which it has been hired–will go for nought. In fact, the lack of matching of expectation and performance may be the most damaging aspect of a firm's attempt to garner repeat business.

The matching of expectations with performance actually consists of two separate assignments: (1) managing the client's expectations to a level the organization can meet on a sustained basis (Davidow and Uttal, 1989); and (2) communication to the service providers within the organization as to the levels of service which they are expected to provide. The successful organization will accomplish *both* of these objectives simultaneously. Raising client expectations and failing to deliver service to that level is a sure path to disaster. Likewise, defining excellent service levels internally without letting the clients know about it is an ineffective method of marketing good services as well as running costs up without a concomitant ability to raise fees. The key is to identify techniques which will simultaneously define client expectations and crystalize performance levels. Since service marketing is a comparatively new field, there is not an abundance of information available on service marketing techniques. We can gain some insight by examining how sellers of tangible goods approach these same questions.

At first blush, the task of managing expectations for consumers of tangible products seems easy. The consumer can see, feel, and often test the product before purchasing it; the prospect for services can do none of these things. However, as is so often the case in human activity, what seems simple on the surface is actually highly complex. A new field of marketing, known as Symbolic Consumer Behavior has arisen to address the aspects of what makes consumers tick at depths below the surface.

In two seminal articles on the subject, Elizabeth Hirschman stated that two people hearing the same advertisement or seeing the same hammer may call into consciousness totally different associations (Hirschman, 1980a and b). The internal meaning will undoubtedly be different for each person, even though the external stimulus may be the same. "It is possible that we are not all perceiving the same 'bundle of attributes' when we observe a hamburger. Further . . . the attributes associated with the hamburger may not even contribute the bulk of its meaning to the consumer" (Hirschman, 1980a). According to the theory of Symbolic Consumer Behavior, the physical attributes of a product have relatively little meaning to the consumer compared to its intangible aspects–packaging, advertising messages, where it is sold, the reputation of the seller and manufacturer.

The sellers of tangible products thus face much the same problem as the sellers of services–how to manage customer expectations with respect to intangible attributes. A widely used approach to this problem is the product warranty or guarantee. Many retailers have long based their principal marketing efforts upon their warranty policies. Craftsman tools are sold by Sears, Roebuck & Co. with a lifetime replacement warranty. If the tool *ever* breaks, Sears replaces it. Period. And Sears has, from time to time, heavily advertised this fact. Many customers will buy no other brand of tools because they enjoy the peace of mind and assurance of quality conveyed by that Craftsman warranty.

Product warranties and guarantees are old hat in product sales. They are less common in service businesses, but they form the basis for some success stories. Federal Express is noted for its promise, "when it absolutely, positively has to get there overnight." But what does this guarantee really encompass? If Federal Express fails to deliver on time, they simply refund the fee for the botched delivery–a few dollars at most. To the customer, however, the promise–and the advertisements which communicate that promise–convey a strong assurance of quality service and a caring attitude about the customer's problems. H & R Block advertises that if they make a mistake on your tax return that requires you to pay more tax, they will pay the interest and penalties due on that return. Block knows that the vast majority of the returns they prepare are so simple that the probability of error is slight, yet the customers receive assurance that H & R Block and its employees really care about what happens to them as customers, and the firm is willing to stand behind its work.

Both of the above guarantees, while subject to significant conditions, are fully functional. Both firms pay on them from time to time, as neither firm has 100 percent perfect performance. The guarantees serve the purpose of reassuring clients that the failure of the organization to perform up to standard will not result in cost to the customer. And, at least as important, the guarantees communicate to employees in the organization: (1) what the firm's performance standards shall be; (2) that substandard performance bears an organizational price; and (3) that repeated lapses by employees from performance standards cannot and will not be tolerated. In the above cases, the use of guarantees is a powerful tool for the firms' managements to use to match customer expectations with performance by their employees.

An even more compelling use of guarantees is presented in a case history in Christopher Hart's article on unconditional service guarantees (Hart, 1988). "Bugs" Burger Bug Killers ("BBBK"), a Miami-based commercial exterminator whose clientele consists principally of restaurants and hotels, has such an unconditional guarantee. While most exterminators claim they will reduce pests to some defined acceptable level, BBBK promises to eliminate them *entirely.* Its Service Guarantee:

1. The customer makes no payment until all pests have been eliminated.

2. If BBBK fails to eliminate all pests, it will refund up to 12 months of fees and will pay for another exterminator for a year.

3. If a guest spots a pest, BBBK will pay for that guest's meal or room, send the guest a letter of apology, and pay for a future meal or room for that guest.

4. If the premises are closed due to roaches or rodents, BBBK will pay all fines and lost profits, plus $5,000.

In short, BBBK says if they do not satisfy their clients 100 percent, they do not want compensation. Period.

Is the BBBK unconditional guarantee a success? The firm operates all over the United States, charges fees up to ten times those of its competitors, and has a disproportionately high market share in the areas in which it operates. In 1986, it paid guarantee claims of $120,000 on sales of $33 million, or about one-third of 1 percent (Hart, 1988). This certainly strikes me as successful.

An unconditional service guarantee helps market services by eliminating what computer people call the "FUD Factor"–Fear, Uncertainty, and Doubt. Services cannot be test driven before they are bought, so there is often a high risk factor in choosing a service provider. Many services can be used only once and not returned after use, as discussed in Chapter 11. An unconditional guarantee, bolstered by a reputation for delivering high-quality service, will go far in alleviating the FUD Factor, for new clients as well as existing ones (Heskett, Sasser, and Hart, 1990). Delta Dental Plan has recently adopted a "Guarantee of Service Excellence" which "gives the purchaser some peace of mind because they can purchase the insurance without worrying about service. . . " (Miller, 1994). In a laboratory experiment on product warranties, however, Innis and Unnava (1991) showed that strong warranties positively affect evaluations only for new brands, but have little effect on established ones; this experiment causes some concern about warranties. However, I believe that the experiment needs replication before its conclusions should be accepted as such. What makes a good guarantee? It is unconditional, easy to understand and communicate, meaningful, easy to invoke, and easy and quick to collect on (Hart, 1988). One must avoid provisions which vitiate the effect of the guarantee.

Guarantees can do three things for the organization, if properly implemented. First, as already mentioned, they can serve notice to the service providers in the organization that there are standards of service that must be met. And there is little point in setting these standards too low; the customers will soon be aware that, although the firm meets its standards, say, 95 percent of the time, its standards do not mean much in the real world. Standards should be attainable, but should require consistently good levels of performance. And the standards should be based on attributes of the service which the clients feel are important, not necessarily ones which the service provider feels are important. Here again, perceptual maps are useful for determining what customers feel is important.

Second, unconditional service guarantees can focus the attention of the organization on areas of its business where service–in the everyday definition of the word–should have a major impact. Often, executives claim that they could not possibly offer an unconditional guarantee. In fact, in the issue of *Harvard Business Review* after Hart's article appeared, there were several letters to the editor about why the concept was fallacious. Bruce Henderson (Professor of Management at Vanderbilt University), after quoting a personal story about how Sears' unconditional guarantee on batteries made him a loyal Sears customer for years, stated that such a guarantee would "appear to be an invitation to unlimited liability in an era of runaway litigation and megabuck damage awards." Creating an unconditional service guarantee "requires an equation that optimizes the relationship between cost, benefits, feasibility, and sustainability of and shifts in competitive advantage" (Henderson, 1988:172). Henderson seems to take the same dismal view of customers that many businesspeople have. Every time I mention the concept of unconditional service guarantees with clients or prospects or other service providers, I hear, "It'll never work; everyone will claim against the guarantee." Yet remember the Burger Bug Killer example above: $120,000 in claims against $33 million in sales–hardly "everyone." Burger is not unique. Several years ago, Piedmont Airlines gave their front-line personnel the authority to write free tickets for lost luggage and ticketing snafus; the finance people claimed that the airline would be bankrupt in short order. According to Donald Shanks, Vice President of Customer Relations, the dollar amount of free tickets *declined* when people were *immediately* offered the ticket as opposed to having to wait for satisfaction (Shanks, 1985). In fact, most customers will be reluctant to press a claim beyond a reasonable amount when faced with immediate satisfaction for that claim. This is the key–immediate, on the spot, no waiting, no questions asked except for clarification of how the snafu happened.

Third, guarantees can provide marketing impact to a firm, particularly if the firm is the first in a market to offer such a guarantee. The odds of gaining powerful marketing impact from such a guarantee are in one's favor when one or more of the following conditions can be met (Hart, 1988):

1. The price of the service is high. Although most professional-service providers' hourly rates are not necessarily high by objective standards, to many clients the idea of charging for time by the hour makes the bills *seem* high.

2. The customer's ego is on the line.

3. The customer's expertise with the service is low. Most people hire professionals either because they cannot or will not perform those services themselves.

4. The negative consequences of service failure are high. Tax audits and will contests are no fun.

5. The industry has a bad image for service quality.

6. The company depends on frequent rebuys from the same customers. Many services do depend on ongoing relationships with the same clients for success, even if not strictly defined "rebuys."

7. The company's business is affected deeply by word of mouth. The statistics of complaint behavior on the part of dissatisfied customers have entered the folklore of business. In one study on durable goods, 54 percent of the dissatisfied buyers said they would not purchase again and 45 percent said they warned a friend against purchase (Hawkins, Best, and Coney, 1986). Study after study has indicated that many times more people go away mad (and tell their friends) than complain to the company. A customer will tell many more people about a bad experience than about a good experience. Virtually *any* business can be deeply affected by word of mouth, and a new service can be quickly crippled by bad word of mouth.

The purpose of an unconditional service guarantee is not to lower consumer complaints and the costs associated with those complaints. The entire objective is to *increase* complaints. In a study of consumers of grocery products, 540 consumers recalled 1,307 separate unsatisfactory purchases; 25 of these purchases resulted in brand switching, 19 percent caused the shopper to stop buying the product. However, only 3 percent complained to the manufacturer, 5 percent complained to the retailer, and 35 percent returned the item. *58 percent did nothing!* The manufacturer has no way of knowing to change these grocery items if no one tells the firm why they do not like them (Hawkins, Best, and Coney, 1986:693) This is why the guarantee must be unconditional, meaningful to the customer, and easy to apply for. The more obstacles the complaining customer encounters, the more likely is that customer to keep quiet—and that is the worst thing that can happen to a business. Lost business is hard to replace; it is doubly hard when one has no idea why it is lost, and at least doubly hard again when one does not even know it is lost for some time afterwards.

No one enjoys listening to client complaints, but we must listen to customers if we are to have any chance at all of improving the services provided so that clients will want to continue to buy them in the future. In a preliminary study comparing responses to dissatisfaction with products and services, the authors state that despite a more knowledgeable and "upscale" sample than the general population, there was "no clear consensus [by respondents] on what action to take in response to unsatisfactory experiences," particularly "once a direct appeal to the [individual] service provider is unsuccessful" (Levy and Suprenant, 1982). A special client-service "hot-line" with a telephone number to the president's office (an 800 number if necessary) will give clients a "clear consensus on what action to take"–quick, easy, and an opportunity to seek redress. And people *will* call.

How is an unconditional service guarantee implemented? The five steps are as follows:

1. Senior management must decide to pay the price, both monetary and psychic, for installing such a guarantee. The entire organization must be refocused toward total commitment to the concept, in a complete transformation of the firm's culture. Without this

commitment, any "tinkering" with an unconditional guarantee will only raise the firm's cost of meeting the guarantee without any of the financial benefits which should accrue, as already discussed. And the psychic cost will probably be at least as great as the monetary costs, as all of a sudden services which in the past were perceived by management as good and well delivered will start to generate meaningful complaints. These complaints will certainly sting.

2. The firm must conduct market research, including surveys, focus groups, interviews with existing clients, interviews with former clients, etc., to determine several things. First, what are clients' perceptions of the firm now? Is it seen as responsive and a top-caliber service provider? Second, what lines of business do clients see as important? Is the firm providing these lines? Do clients know this? It is at this point that offering a "limited" service guarantee first becomes possible. If it seems impossible to guarantee everything about all the lines of service which the firm provides, a limited guarantee for limited lines is better than nothing at all and may show the way for the firm to expand the guarantee at a later date.

3. The firm must train its employees. This is not limited to training to raise technical competence; clients have a right to expect competence from service providers and firms have an incentive (lower incidence of error-caused claims) to insist on technical competence from their employees. Henderson is correct about the litigious nature of clients. However, given the fact that there is at least an implicit guarantee on services imposed by the courts if not by the provider, it would behoove the service provider to train its employees to inculcate a sensitivity to the needs of being on the frontline for client service.

This is a new role for many service providers–especially professionals–but it is a crucial role. The service provider becomes critical in delivering client satisfaction. For products, the reliance on retailers is overwhelming–almost 90 percent of the initial responses to dissatisfaction cited above involved returning the product to the retailer. This dominance is not so clear-cut for services; however, "complaining to the provider is still the most popular initial action" (Levy and Suprenant, 1982). When we remember the statement by Levy and Suprenant mentioned above that those surveyed did not receive a clear sense of how to appeal from the service providers, the importance of this training becomes indisputable, as does the need to clarify the paths of appeal.

4. The firm must commit to stay close to what the clients want. Forever. This will necessitate establishing quantitative and qualitative measures to ensure that the new outlook of the firm is translated into procedures that allow the firm to continue the unconditional guarantee (*Close to the Customer,* 1987)–adhering to the Marketing Concept and continual perceptual mapping of the market. Although this is similar to the statement in item 1 above, it is not identical. This is where the essence of being a "client-centered" or "market-driven" firm enters; one's clients will henceforth dictate what the firm provides, not the firm itself, or the firm will not survive long-term.

5. The firm must determine what to guarantee. The answer: whatever it is in the services provided which *clients find to be most important.* To BBBK's customers, it is the complete freedom from vermin. To an accountant's clients, it might be "no penalties from IRS audits." To a consultant's clients, it might be timely delivery of all reports. By warranting that which the client deems crucial, the service provider will perforce be aiming the quality effort in the correct direction. Again, this seems similar to item 3 above, but it has a different focus. The focus here is again on the *client's* desires. It is not on "what can the firm do" but rather on "what the clients need."

In summary, we have seen how a service organization can, through the careful design and communication of a service guarantee, manage the expectations of its clients to a level that the firm can consistently meet, and also convey to the employees a clear sense of purpose and expected levels of performance. To the extent such a guarantee is limited by various conditions, it loses much of its effectiveness for such purposes. An unconditional service guarantee packs the greatest punch and delivers the most forceful message to clients and employees alike. And, while the cost of an unconditional guarantee may well exceed that of a conditional guarantee, the cost would fade into insignificance when compared with the resulting gains in revenues and profitability. Remember BBBK's $120,000 expense on $33 million of revenue. It is critical to the successful implementation of a guarantee program that management be fully committed to bear the costs in terms of market research, employee training, and warranty claims themselves. The unconditional service guarantee offers a unique opportunity to create a successful service organization for the firms who have the foresight to implement such a guarantee.

Chapter 13

Conclusion

So, now that we approach the end of the course, where are we? I have attempted to lay out two hoary, long-lived but often-forgotten tools–the Marketing Concept and perceptual mapping–onto the workbench of the marketer who seeks to introduce a new service. I have employed several examples to show how to use these tools, as well as what can happen when they are not used at all or are inadequately applied. Further, I have spent time discussing a third tool–unconditional service guarantees–which can be successfully applied as a means of establishing a differential marketing advantage, whether the firm is introducing a new service or not. And last, but certainly not least, I have entered a plea to manage innovation and innovativeness with a view to innovating only as much as the customers want, not to fill some sort of organizational need, real or perceived. What are we left with? A cleft stick, with management firmly caught in the cleft. On one side is "me-tooism" of the offerings, and on the other is what I have always called "Missionary Marketing."

"Me-tooism" is, obviously, the look-alike service, or what in computer software is called the "look-and-feel" problem. Many years ago there was a television advertisement, I think it was for Xerox copiers, where a salesman slithered into an office and asked the manager to buy his copier because it was "just as good as a Xerox. . . . " This is me-tooism of the first water. What marketing points does me-tooism allow? Few indeed for a product and fewer still for a service. An obvious point is lower price. The full quotation from the Xerox commercial ran, I believe, "It's just as good as a Xerox, only cheaper."

I have hardly mentioned price in this book–for a good reason. I am not a believer in price competition. To again paraphrase a line from Isaac Asimov's *Foundation* series of books, "Price competition is the last refuge of the incompetent." Anyone can sell more by cutting the price of the goods and services offered. However, only the lowest-cost producer can survive a long-term price war, and even the lowest-cost producer may be grievously injured by such action.

When I taught a marketing case course to graduate students, one of the cases inevitably led the case analyst to suggest cutting the price of the goods offered by the firm. Cutting price as a competitive weapon is not only easy to copy, but it is almost inevitably, invariably, copied by one's competitors. Do they have any choice? Thus, sales at a lower price do not gain a competitive edge, do not buy market share, but only lower revenue and profit for the firm (and the industry) after the dust settles. No action by the firm will occur in a vacuum; *competitive reaction must always be taken into account.*

This is not to say that pricing of the new service is not important; setting the price is extremely important to the long-term success of the new offering. And mishandling of the initial pricing decisions can kill the new offering immediately, or cripple it in the marketplace for years (Cahill, 1994b). It is tempting for a me-too product or service to be introduced as "just as good as a Xerox, only cheaper." I would like to pass along a "me-too" service idea where the price is equal to or greater than the competition's but the cost to the customer is lower, which combination should lead to greater sales at higher profits for the new service.

Suppose one desired to start a new airline service–a service which, given the realities of the airline business, operates at similar fares to what competitors offered. A new airline which entered a market at lower fares would probably find those fares matched by better-known airlines and thus, the attempt to buy market share would probably fail. And yet, suppose that the airline cut a wholesale deal with a local taxi company to offer coupons to its customers for free cab rides to the airport included in the ticket price. The deal would allow the cab company to schedule its taxis for better utilization, since the company would know who was leaving at what time and could arrange pickups ahead of time, reducing the cruising time of its cabs. I live a $25-cab-ride from the airport; if the airline ticket price were $15 more than the competition, but saved me the $25 cab fare, I would take the new airline. If the cab ride cost the airline less than $15 (possible, if the cab company could be made to understand the economics of the wholesale purchasing of rides), everyone would win. And this would be a very difficult marketing strategy for the airline's competition to match.

If the cab example seems a bit theoretical, the following is a true case of a retailer's creative pricing to help establish an unusual service package. There is a locally owned chain of tire stores in Cleveland which has recently started advertising a new service package–a total approach to selling tires. When a customer buys new tires from them, he or she is given a one-year unconditional guarantee by the store against loss of the tire–the "Complete Tire Protection Plan." If the tire is declared irreparable because of road-hazard damage–and Cleveland's streets are nothing *but* road hazards by the end of winter–during the first year, it is replaced free; during the second year, it is replaced at half-price. Further, every 5,000 miles the customer is entitled to free rotation of the tire–for its life. "It's like buying a new suit and getting free cleaning, and if you rip it, you get a new suit," to quote the radio advertisement.

How successful has this program been? It is too early to tell (although by the end of the 1993/1994 winter, the firm was advertising 12 free replacements daily), but the program offers an interesting instance of raising the customer's price (for this chain is emphatically *not* the lowest-price retailer–in fact it is a premium-priced retailer) while lowering the cost to the customer. The free rotation is worth more than $50.00 per year (based on four tires to be rotated and 10,000 miles driven each year)–about the price of one of this chain's low-end tires. The premium price charged allows the store to bear the additional labor cost of doing what the customer should have done. And, of course, some of the cost of replacing tires ruined by road hazards will be reimbursed to the store by the tire manufacturer's warranty.

What does the chain stand to gain by offering this new level of service warranty? They gain more sales per customer over time as customers realize the added benefits to them of this new package, and probably more customers overall. The chain has lowered the life-cycle cost of buying tires, even though the purchase price is *not* the lowest in town.

Be creative with pricing instead of simply using price cutting as the way to enter a new market, or market a new service. However, being creative does not mean ignoring some rules of thumb about how to price that have been derived from experience and theory. A common misconception is that price equals the value of a service; at best it equals the value as perceived by the buyer. Failure to understand how customers perceive value and price leads to three major errors (Monroe, 1993):

1. Not distinguishing between perceived value and price
2. Not distinguishing between absolute price and relative price
3. Not distinguishing between pricing strategies and pricing tactics.

And, to further whet the creative-pricing juices, Alpert, Wilson, and Elliott (1993) discuss "price signalling," which they define as using the price–generally a price higher than competitors' prices–of a good or service to let customers know that it is of greater "quality" than the competitors' offerings. The airline example cited above shows a theoretical method by which such price signalling might work.

The "me-too" service also can be offered with better hours. Doctors and dentists have traditionally had office hours that suited *them* rather than their patients. Recently clinics and group practices have extended hours to the evening and on weekends as a competitive device. This also counters the moves by the urgent-care centers, and the movement of such offerings into stores such as Sears which keep the traditional retailers' hours. Moving location from the traditional office buildings to shopping malls was another way to compete by offering a "me-too" service in a decidedly different location. But the four Ps of product (service), place, price, and promotion can all be matched by competitors who are willing to take the steps necessary to match them, even if this means lowering what have been higher margins. It is better to have lower margins than none at all. The only conclusion is that "me-tooism" does not work; the only salvation is to have the unique service, one which forces the competition to duplicate the service, however difficult a task this may prove to be in the end.

This leads management into the other cleft of the stick: "Missionary Marketing." "Missionary Marketing" is a term which I define as marketing a product or service by spending most of your time telling customers what it is that the product does. The story of *CompuAd/NewsAd* is a case in point. Every trade show, every sales call, every presentation I was involved in with *CompuAd* led to the same question from real estate agents: "Isn't this just like my phrase book?" Agents frequently make use of phrase books to help write their classifieds; in fact, one of the Chairman's colleagues from the National Association of Real Estate Publishers published a $15 phrase book and sold it at the same trade shows as the $300 + *NewsAd*–on one awful occasion, directly opposite the DECOY booth. Our response was always: "No, *NewsAd* is *not* a phrase book; it is actually writing the advertisement as you watch, based upon research which has determined the priorities buyers have toward house features." Agents tended not to understand, nor certainly care much about, the difference between *NewsAd* and a phrase book (although they certainly *did* care about the difference between $15 and the more-than $300 for *NewsAd*).

But this lack of understanding and caring extended far beyond the level of the real estate agent. A presentation we made to Coldwell Banker, attended by several vice presidents and assistant vice presidents, suffered from the same lack of understanding and caring. The frequent response by technologically savvy people–but not the people who would actually have to do the programming–was that *NewsAd* looked simple and that they could certainly duplicate it in a few weeks. *NewsAd* does look simple in operation, and it seems to act like a computerized phrase book; however, the research which has gone into the software has been going on for almost two decades. It suffers from the apparent ease from which an All-Star shortstop suffers: it makes it look easy.

Missionary Marketing can be debilitating. An organization spends too much time and too many resources telling everyone what the service does and why everyone should have at least one, and too little time selling. Rejection is a mild term for the total lack of comprehension that too often confront marketing efforts. And yet, often a truly innovative service–such as *NewsAd* or Federal Express–will force an organization to enter a campaign of Missionary Marketing because no one has any idea what the service is or what one can accomplish with it.

There are times when a firm must employ missionary marketing, and it may be successful; one of the most obvious of these times is when a totally new product or service is offered. High technology companies have practiced the art for years; when Intel invented the microprocessor, no one (including Intel) quite knew what to do with it, so missionaries from Intel went around to potential users and gave them chips and information so they could develop applications (Jelinek and Schoonhoven, 1993). Apple called these people "evangelists" and sent them out to spread the word that the Macintosh was "insanely great" and that thousands of the machines were going to be sold; therefore anyone who wrote programs for the machine would get rich or famous or both and everyone should jump on the bandwagon.

Guy Kawasaki, probably the most famous and successful of Apple's evangelists, wrote a book entitled *Selling the Dream* wherein he defines evangelism as "the process of convincing people to believe in your product or idea as much as you do. It means selling your dream by using fervor, zeal, guts, and cunning" (1991:3). He continues in the rest of the book to discuss how evangelism can work to sell almost anything. And I believe he is correct. I object to Missionary Marketing when it is used to sell only part of the firm's line; Kawasaki describes building the entire firm around evangelism from the beginning. Most firms seem to undertake Missionary Marketing only when all else has failed, and they have developed a new something that requires it before anyone will buy the item the firm offers.

The first true spreadsheet program for personal computers–VisiCalc–was a raging success for the small firm which wrote it (Software Arts) and the small firm which sold it (VisiCorp) primarily because the people who bought a spreadsheet program in the early days of personal computers knew what a paper-and-pencil spreadsheet was and what it could do; the authors of the program wrote it originally while they were studying for MBAs. All VisiCalc needed to tell its customers to get them to buy it was that it was an electronic spreadsheet which would do the work of the paper-and-pencil spreadsheet quicker without them having to enter data into an electronic calculator. The early word processing programs were sold to people who were already typists and, thus, knew what sorts of operations they would like to have a machine perform to lessen the drudgery of certain kinds of typing.

How do you sell something which no one but the originator has conceived as necessary or useful? This has been part of *CompuAd's* problem. It was the downfall of the *AdWriter* machine. It was part of *Locus's* problem. It was part of InfoVision's problem. Solutions to problems that customers do not realize they have can go begging for years, if not decades. How do you sell deodorant if body odor is not seen as a problem? Mouthwash if "halitosis" is an unknown concept? Overnight small-package delivery in a country where two- or three-day delivery is considered adequate? Obviously, through Missionary Marketing. One must, however, think of Missionary Marketing as a strategic alternative, not a means of quickly selling thousands of instances of the service. It will not happen; Federal Express was not an overnight success.

Missionary Marketing becomes even more problematical in a business-to-business setting, and even worse when the new service requires the purchaser to change the way he or she organizes work. As Bikson, Gutek, and Mankin report (1981), the consensus from previous research is that "recognition of a technological opportunity in the absence of a clear organizational need to be served by such innovation is not likely to lead to successful implementation." This was part of the *AdWriter* machine's problem, and always has been part of *CompuAd's* difficulty. As one real estate office's secretary said when an *AdWriter* was placed in her office: "Why should I have to enter all this data when the *Locus* office already does this for us?"

As part of the introduction of the newspaper to the real estate community, anyone who wished to have *CompuAd* write ads for them–and part of the Cleveland real estate community knew *CompuAd*–and save themselves the bother of counting lines and characters to get the advertising copy to fit within *Locus's* standard ad space, could send what was then called the Data Assembler Form down to the *Locus* office with all of the information filled in, and *Locus* personnel would input the data and produce the advertisement for the agent. Many offices encouraged their agents to participate in this service. When *AdWriters* were placed in "friendly" offices for a test, DECOY, Inc.'s, people had forgotten that *Locus* was providing this service in Cleveland, and one of the offices selected turned out to be a big user of *Locus*'s input service.

This leads to the next point that management needs to focus on during the introduction of new services: the interaction among existing offerings and the new offerings. I have already alluded to the fact that dropping a new service into an existing market will make the existing competitors react; this was always difficult to get MBA students to grasp, but practiced managers understand this fact completely. Offering a new service will force other parts of the offering firm to react to the new offering, often in ways that can prove to be embarrassing or costly, as the example above between *Locus* and the *AdWriter* show. Taking over someone else's offering can cause similar problems, whether the organization is a for-profit entity, a not-for-profit entity, or a public enterprise (Ingersoll and Adams, 1992).

In my experience, both as a consultant and as a teacher, this interaction among offerings and among competitors is probably the most overlooked aspect of new product or service introduction. Planning may be a difficult undertaking (one author has delightfully named his attack on planning *Managing the Unknowable* [Stacey, 1992]); however, failing to account for possible changes in the firm's current offerings because of the introduction of new services–even if they seem not to have any interrelation–can be catastrophic and is a simple-minded failing, one which can be overcome by thorough thinking through implications of actions. Existing product or service managers can be quickly interviewed to ascertain what they plan to do with their product or service when the introduction of the new one is made. I will bet almost anything that they will react somehow. And the firm's outside competitors will certainly react to a new offering, particularly in a crowded market.

Recently, a new bicycle shop opened in my area; the proprietor called me in advance to let me know about it. Frank had been the mechanic at the local shop and had kept my old Peugeot ten-speed–a wedding present from my wife–going, despite my pedalling 2,500 miles per year. The proprietor of the existing bike shop is known to be "difficult," but runs a good store. Frank decided that although the area probably did not "need" another shop, he would squeeze his in anyhow. His differentiating factor (aside from not being "difficult")? He will pick up your bike at no charge to take it to his shop for repairs, which will be done at the same price as at the existing shop. How successful has he been? It is too early to tell, but his innovative introduction has been well received.

Competitors' reactions may be slow; American management in many markets has been castigated for the past several years for being slow to react to outside threats. Some of that chastisement is warranted–particularly in steel and autos–and some is not. But any management which seeks to introduce a new service into a crowded market and fails to take into account the probable actions of the competition in that crowded market–whether internal or external–is guilty of a lapse of managerial competence that should be grounds for termination. Has Frank's former employer reacted to the new competition? Absolutely. He is advertising more than before and gave his employees a raise to keep them from leaving.

What about advertising the new service? We have made it almost all the way to the end of the journey without a mention of advertising services, only about three media whose revenues consisted of advertising. Spending money on advertising may be necessary when trying to squeeze the new service into a crowded market; however, advertising is certainly no panacea. Stern (1988) makes the point that special care needs to be taken when devising advertisements for services: tangibilizing the intangible, making a complex offering clear to the consumer, differentiating one offering from another. Figurative language is important.

Hill and Gandhi (1992) make two important points about services advertising. First, when customers go to service organizations, their confidence in the service would be enhanced if they could visualize the service beforehand–a plus for television advertising if ever there was one. But note that they do not say "visualize the service provider"; I guess this means that the television ads featuring the owners of dental and legal clinics are not terribly germane to what customers need. Second, customers need to know about availability of outlets, given the fact that services tend to be tied to the sites where they are provided. The sum and substance of these two articles is that simply shouting louder (even better) than the rest of the market players may not be enough to gain success.

Thus, at the end of the journey, we are left with some tools to use in determining what the new service offering should be, where it should be offered, to whom, and how: the Marketing Concept and perceptual mapping. And we are left with a powerful tool to use in helping to shape the new service offering: unconditional guarantees. These tools are only as good as the craftsman or craftswoman who uses them. They are tools powerful enough to need caution in their use, as they may turn around and bite the hand that uses them carelessly. Particularly the Marketing Concept, for one must exercise extreme and constant vigilance in ensuring that one has determined what the proper market is, and what the correct set of customers or potential customers wants. If one asks the wrong group, the wrong result pops up. And as my late finance professor was fond of saying, "An estimate divided by a guess yields a firm number, so be careful."

As stated in Chapter 12 on unconditional guarantees, the firm must continually stay close to its market, must continue to spend money and time and other resources on market research to endeavor to define its market correctly, to find out what its market truly wants. The radio station I listen to most frequently has had, for about 30 years, a program on Saturday night which consists mostly of comedy records–on an all-classical station. The first Saturday night of the New Year has traditionally been a listener-request program. This year the host announced that instead of the all-request program, he was having a "No request all request" program, because "I know what you'll ask for anyway." And he proceeded to play some selections that have been requested for those 30 years, plus a few newer ones. This was probably a fair approximation of what the listener-request program would have sounded like; however, it was a dangerous, hubris-ridden effort which could have failed miserably. As Zap-Mail failed for Federal Express. As the Edsel failed for Ford. When one begins to answer for the market, to decide that the market research is no longer needed because "I no what you'll ask for anyway," one rides boldly into danger. Guy Kawasaki's Five-Step Process to get great products is appropriate to quote here–and it also applies to services. Lead the Market, Take a Shot, Listen to the Market, Respond, and Lead Again (Kawasaki, 1991).

Use the tools given here and keep close to the customer. Listen to your customers, whether you really want to or not. Solicit their opinions, their complaints, their praise. Send them newsletters filled with success stories from your customers–and failures, too, if those failures point to potential problems that other customers should avoid. Hold user meetings and ask for suggestions by your users for improvements in your offerings. Von Hippel (1986) is onto something when he suggests getting ideas for new products and services from your customers; take advantage of his research. Love your customers; they pay your salary. I do not mean this in the sense of the sign at Stew Leonard's grocery:

Rule #1: The Customer is always right.

Rule #2: If the Customer is wrong, see Rule #1.

The customer is often wrong; customers often do not understand what it is that you are trying to do. But it is not their fault that they are ignorant; it is your fault. And your golden opportunity. Educate them. Educate them to your service in a way that your competition cannot or will not, and they will not leave you. Take care of them when they need help and they will be grateful and stay with you for years. Given the risks inherent in trying new services, service customers should be inherently more loyal than product customers (see Jackson, 1985, for a discussion of keeping customers).

I am often amazed at the customer-provider relationship that seems to transcend rational analysis. It *is* often based on emotion. As previously mentioned, early in my career I worked in credit and collections for the Medusa Cement Company; several times I heard, or read on credit applications, of firms who would always buy from Medusa (or a competitor) because of something done 30 years earlier. Or, of course, the firms who would *never* buy from us because of something deleterious that was done years earlier. These kinds of relationships need to be nurtured, not taken for granted as they usually are. The loyal customer needs to be rewarded, and cosseted as the airlines understood when they started the Frequent Flyer programs. These are the customers to kill for.

Above all, as one of my marketing professors said years ago, "Keep the Marketing Concept uppermost in your mind and you cannot go too far wrong." I concur.

References

Aaker, David A. and George S. Day. (1986). "The Perils of High-growth Markets." *Strategic Management Journal,* pp. 409-421.

Alpert, Frank. (1987). "Product Categories, Product Hierarchy, and Pioneership: A Consumer Behavior Explanation for Pioneer Brand Advantage." In Susan P. Douglas, Vijah Mahajan, William M. Pride, Gary T. Ford, Peter Doyle, Michael R. Solomon, Mark I. Alpert, Gary L. Frazier, and James C. Anderson (eds.), *1987 AMA Educators' Proceedings.* Chicago: American Marketing Association, pp. 133-138.

_____ , Beth Wilson, and Michael T. Elliott. (1993). "Price Signalling: Does It Ever Work?" *Pricing Strategy & Practice*, Volume 1, No. 3, pp. 20-30.

Alsop, Stewart. (1992). "Sometimes You Can Do Without the Bells and Whistles." *InfoWorld,* January 20, p. 4.

American LIVES. (1991). "Study of the Denver Real Estate Market."

Asimov, Isaac. (1951). *Foundation.* New York: Doubleday.

Berry, Dick. (1988). "The Marketing Concept Revisited: It's Setting Goals, Not Making a Mad Dash for Profits." *Marketing News,* July 18, pp. 26, 28.

Berry, Leonard L. and A. Parasuraman. (1991). *Marketing Services: Competing Through Quality.* New York: The Free Press.

Berton, Lee. (1989). "Innovating Means Taking Time From Same Old Grind." *The Wall Street Journal,* August 31, p. B2.

Bikson, Tora K., Barbara A. Gutek, and Don A. Mankin. (1981). "Implementation of Information Technology in Office Settings: Review of Relevant Literature." The Rand Corporation, P-6697.

Bleasdale, Julie A. (1991). "FSBO's Comments Echo Industry Research." *Real Estate Today,* May, p. 17.

Bordessa, Ronald. (1979a). "The Residential Broker as Country Gentleman." *Real Estate Review,* Fall, pp. 94-99.

_____. (1979b). "Rhetoric versus Reality in Residential Real Estate Brokerage." *Real Estate Review,* Winter, pp. 98-101.

Brown, Anne. (1987). "Polish Your Professional Image." *Real Estate Today,* August, pp. 36-38.

Brown, Rick. (1992). "Managing the 'S' Curves of Innovation." *The Journal of Consumer Marketing,* Winter, pp. 61-72.

Bulkeley, William M. (1994). "Semi-Prose, Perhaps, But Sportswriting by Software Is a Hit." *The Wall Street Journal,* March 29, pp. A1, A5.

Burke, Raymond R., Arvind Rangaswamy, Jerry Wind, and Jehoshua Eliashberg. (1988). "ADCAD: A Knowledge-Based System for Advertising Design." Working Paper #88-027. Philadelphia: Wharton School of the University of Pennsylvania.

Business Plan, *Cleveland Edition.* (1986).

Cahill, Dennis J. (1990). "Industrializing Services: An Example of What Not to Do." In *Stayin' Alive Through '95: How to Thrive and Not Just Survive,* Proceedings of the 9th Annual Services Marketing Conference. Chicago: American Marketing Association, pp. 52-63.

_____. (1992). "I Want a Choice, Not the 'Standard' Excuse." *Marketing News,* January 6, pp. 4, 32.

_____. (1994a). "A Two-Stage Model of the Search Process for Single-Family Houses: A Research Note." *Environment and Behavior,* January, pp. 38-48.

_____. (1994b). "Pricing: How Not To Succeed." *Pricing Strategy and Tactics,* Vol. 2(1), pp. 21-26..

Cahill, Dennis J. and Robert M. Warshawsky. (1993). "The Marketing Concept: A Forgotten Aid for Marketing High-Technology Products." *Journal of Consumer Marketing,* Volume 10, No. 1, pp. 17-22.

Cahill, Dennis J., Sharon V. Thach, and Robert M. Warshawsky. (1994). "From Experience: The Marketing Concept and New High-Tech Products: Is There a Fit?" *Journal of Product Innovation Management,* Vol. 11(4), pp. 336-343.

Calantone, Roger J. and Robert G. Cooper. (1977). "A Typology of Industrial New Products." In Barrett A. Greenberg and Danny N. Ballenger (eds.), *Contemporary Marketing Thought.* (Chicago: American Marketing Association), pp. 492-497.

Carlson, Eugene. (1993). "Farmers Reap New Business with Crop of Inventions." *The Wall Street Journal,* January 29, p. B2.

Carpenter, Gregory S. and Kent Nakamoto. (1988). "Market Pioneering, Learning, and Preference" In Michael J. Houston (ed.), *Advances in Consumer Research, XV.* Provo, UT: Association for Consumer Research, pp. 275-279.

Clandinin, D. Jean and F. Michael Connelly. (1994). "Personal Experience Methods" In Norman K. Denzin and Yvonna S. Lincoln (eds.), *Handbook of Qualitative Research.* Thousand Oaks, CA: Sage, pp. 413-427.

Close to the Customer: An American Management Association Research Report on Consumer Affairs. (1987). Chicago: AMACOM.

Cooper, Lee G. (1983). "A Review of Multidimensional Scaling in Marketing Research." Working paper, Graduate School of Management, University of California at Los Angeles.

Cooper, R. G. (1979). "The Dimensions of Industrial New Product Success and Failure." *Journal of Marketing,* pp. 93-103.

_____. (1986). *Winning at New Products.* Reading, MA: Addison-Wesley.

Cooper, R. G. (1987). "New Products: What Separates Winners from Losers?" *Journal of Marketing,* pp. 169-184.

_____. (1993). *Winning at New Products: Accelerating the Process from Idea to Launch,* 2nd edition. Reading, MA: Addison-Wesley.

Cooper, R. G. and Ulricke de Brentanis. (1991). "New Industrial Financial Services: What Distinguishes the Winners." *Journal of Marketing,* pp. 75-90.

Cooper, R. G. and E. J. Kleinschmidt. (1993). "Major New Products: What Distinguishes the Winners in the Chemical Industry?" *Journal of Marketing,* pp. 90-111.

Crawford, John C. (1983). "The Marketing Concept–A Utopian Dream?" In John C. Rogers, III (ed.), *Developments in Marketing Science VI.* Logan, UT: Academy of Marketing Science, pp. 450-452.

Crawford, C. Merle. (1977). "Marketing Research and the New Product Failure Rate." *Journal of Marketing,* April, pp. 51-61.

Crockett, John H. (1984). "Price Competition for Residential Brokerage." *Real Estate Review,* Winter, pp. 98-101.

Dauw, Dean C. (1969), "Bridging the Creativity-Innovation Gap." *The Journal of Creative Behavior,* pp. 84-89.

Davidow, William H. and Bro Uttal. (1989). "Service Companies: Focus or Falter." *Harvard Business Review,* July-August, pp. 75- 85.

DECOY, Inc. (1986a). "Memo."

_____. (1986b). "A Closer Look at DECOY's Electronic Marketing System for Residential Real Estate: The *CompuAd/AdWriter* System and the HomeSight Mall Marketing System."

Dholakia, Ruby Roy and Meera Venkatraman. (1993). "Marketing Services that Compete with Goods." *Journal of Services Marketing,* Volume 7 No. 2, pp. 16-23.

Dietz, Jim and Richard May. (1993). "A Conversation at Sam's Bar: How to Start a Publication with Under $300." *The River Burns,* June, p. 7.

Dolan, Robert J. and John M. Matthews. (1993). "Maximizing the Utility of Customer Product Testing: Beta Test Design and Management." *Journal of Product Innovation Management,* pp. 318-330.

Dooley, Thomas W. and Charles M. Dahlheimer. (1989). *Real Estate in the '90s: A Whole New World Ahead.* St. Louis, MO: North American Consulting Group, Inc.

Drollinger, John M. (1986). "Cleveland *Edition* Market Research: Appendices 5, 6, and 7."

Dunlap, B. J., Michael J. Dotson, and Terry M. Chambers. (1988). "Perceptions of Real Estate Brokers and Buyers: A Sales-Orientation, Customer-Orientation Approach." *Journal of Business Research,* pp. 175-187.

Edmonds, Charles P. and Rudolph Lindbeck. (1987). "How Brokers Can Reduce Vulnerability to Lawsuits." *Real Estate Review,* Spring, pp. 90-93.

Edwards, Mark R. and J. Ruth Sproull. (1984). "Creativity: Productivity Gold Mine?" *The Journal of Creative Behavior,* pp. 175-184.

Evans, Joel R. and Barry Berman. (1987). *Marketing,* 3rd. ed. (New York: Macmillan).

Evans, Joel R. and Blaine Sherman. (1979). "Improving New Product Planning Through an Analysis of New Product Failure." In Howard S. Gitlow and Edward W. Wheatley (eds.), *Develop-

ments in Marketing Science, II. Miami: Academy of Marketing Science, pp. 294-299.

Fox, Isaac and Alfred Marcus. (1992). "The Causes and Consequences of Leveraged Management Buyouts." *Academy of Management Review,* January, pp. 62-85.

Fugate, Douglas L. and L. W. Turley. (1992). "The New Service Development Process: An Assessment." In Victoria L. Crittenden (ed.), *Developments in Marketing Science, XV.* San Diego: Academy of Marketing Science, pp. 454-459.

Gersh, Debra. (1989). "Newspapers and Homes." *Editor & Publisher,* June 3, pp. 26-27.

Gottko, John. (1985). "Marketing Strategy Implications of the Emerging Patterns of Consumer Geographic Mobility." In Robert F. Lusch, Gary T. Ford, Gary L. Frazier, Roy D. Howe, Charles A. Ingene, Michael Reilly, and Ronald W. Sampfl (eds.), *1985 AMA Educators' Proceedings.* Chicago: American Marketing Association, pp. 290-295.

_____. (1986). "Emerging Patterns of Urban Geographic Mobility and Resulting Public Policy Implications." In Terence A. Shimp, Subhash Sharma, George Juhn, John A. Quelch, John H. Lindgren, Jr., William Dillon, Meryl Paula Gardiner, and Robert F. Dyer (eds.), *1986 AMA Educators' Proceedings.* Chicago: American Marketing Association, pp. 363-368.

Grigsby, William G. (1984). "Residential Brokerage Costs Are Too High." *Real Estate Review,* Summer, pp. 109-112.

Grove, Stephen J. and Raymond P. Fisk. (1992). "The Service Experience as Theater." In *Advances in Consumer Research, XIX.* Provo, UT: Association for Consumer Research, pp. 455-461.

_____. (1989). "Impression Management in Services Marketing: A Dramaturgical Perspective." In Robert A. Giacalone and Paul Rosenfeld (eds.), *Impression Management in the Organization.* Hillsdale, NJ: Lawrence Erlbaum Associates, pp. 427-438.

_____ and Mary Jo Bitner. (1992). "Dramatizing the Service Experience: A Managerial Approach." In Teresa A. Swartz, Stephen W. Brown, and David E. Bowen (eds.), *Advances in Services Marketing and Management: Research and Practice.* Greenwich, CT: JAI Press.

Grove, Stephen J., Raymond P. Fisk, and James T. Kenny. (1990). "Personal Selling as Drama: A Metaphorical Assessment of Buyer-Seller Interaction." In David Lichtenthal et al. (eds.), *1990 AMA Winter Educators' Conference: Marketing Theory and Applications.* Chicago: American Marketing Association.

Gupta, Udayan. (1993). "Costly Market Research Pays Off for Biotech Start-Up." *The Wall Street Journal,* August 2, p. B2.

Hampton, Gerald M. and Emmett Lane. (1982). "Newspapers and the Marketing Concept: An Exploratory Study of the Attitudes of Newsroom and Management Personnel." In Vinay Kothari (ed.), *Developments in Marketing Science, V.* Nagodoches, TX: Academy of Marketing Science, pp. 450-455.

Hart, Christopher W. L. (1988). "The Power of Unconditional Service Guarantees." *Harvard Business Review,* July-August, pp. 54-62.

————— , James L. Heskett, and W. Earl Sasser, Jr. (1990). "The Profitable Art of Service Recovery." *Harvard Business Review,* July-August, pp. 148-156.

Hawkins, Del I., Roger J. Best, and Kenneth A. Coney. (1986). *Consumer Behavior: Implications for Marketing Strategy,* 3rd edition. Plano, TX: Business Publications.

Henderson, Bruce. (1988). "Letter." *Harvard Business Review,* September-October, p. 172.

Herstatt, Cornelius and Eric von Hippel. (1992). "Developing New Product Concepts Via the Lead User Method: A Case Study in a 'Low-Tech' Field." *Journal of Product Innovation Management,* pp. 213- 221.

Heskett, James L., W. Earl Sasser, Jr., and Christopher W. L. Hart. (1990). *Service Breakthroughs: Changing the Rules of the Game.* New York: The Free Press.

Higgins, Susan H. and William L. Shanklin. (1992). "Seeking Mass Market Acceptance for High-Technology Products." *The Journal of Consumer Marketing,* Winter, pp. 5-14.

Hill, Donna J. and Nimish Gandhi. (1992). "Services Advertising: A Framework to Its Effectiveness." *Journal of Services Advertising,* Fall, pp. 63-76.

Hirschman, Elizabeth C. (1980a). "Commonality and Idiosyncrasy in Popular Culture: An Empirical Examination of the 'Layers of Meaning' Concept." In Elizabeth C. Hirschman and Morris B.

Holbrook (eds.), *Symbolic Consumer Behavior.* Ann Arbor, MI: Association for Consumer Research, pp. 29-34.

_____. (1980b). "Comprehending Symbolic Consumption." In Elizabeth C. Hirschman and Morris B. Holbrook (eds.), *Symbolic Consumer Behavior.* Ann Arbor, MI: Association for Consumer Research, pp. 4-6.

_____. (1983). "Aesthetics, Ideologies, and the Limits of the Marketing Concept." *Journal of Marketing,* Summer, pp. 45-55.

Horne, David A., John P. McDonald, and David L. Williams. (1986). "Consumer Perception of Service Dimensions: Implications for Marketing Strategy." In M. Venkatesan, Diane M. Schmalensee, and Claudia Marshall (eds.), *Creativity in Services Marketing: What's New, What Works, What's Developing.* Chicago: American Marketing Association, pp. 35-39.

Houston, Michael J. and Seymour Sudman. (1977). "Real Estate Agents as a Source of Information for Home Buyers." *The Journal of Consumer Affairs,* pp. 110-121.

Ingersoll, Virginia Hill and Guy B. Adams. (1992). *The Tacit Organization.* Greenwich, CT: JAI Press, Inc.

Innis, Daniel E. and H. Rao Unnava. (1991). "The Usefulness of Product Warranties for Reputable and New Brands." In Rebecca H. Holman and Michael R. Solomon (eds.), *Advances in Consumer Research, Vol. XVIII.* Provo, UT: Association for Consumer Research, pp. 317-322.

Jackson, Barbara Bund. (1985). *Winning & Keeping Industrial Customers: The Dynamics of Customer Relationships.* Lexington, MA: Lexington Books.

Jelinek, Mariann and Claudia Bird Schoonhoven. (1993). *The Innovation Marathon: Lessons from High Technology Firms.* San Francisco: Jossey-Bass.

Johnston, Christopher. (1992). "Raiders of the Lost Art." *The River Burns,* October, pp. 4-8.

Kawasaki, Guy. (1991). *Selling the Dream: How to Promote Your Product, Company, or Ideas–and Make a Difference–Using Everyday Evangelism.* New York: HarperCollins.

Kleinschmidt, E. J. and R. G. Cooper. (1991). "The Impact of Product Innovativeness on Performance." *Journal of Product Innovation Management,* pp. 240-251.

Kohli, Chiranjeev S. and Lance Leuthesser. (1993). "Product Positioning: A Comparison of Perceptual Mapping Techniques." *The Journal of Product & Brand Management,* Volume 2, No. 4, pp. 10-19.

Kowalysko, Ihor A. (n.d., a). "Analyzing Two-Dimensional MDPREF Configurations Using Non-Parametric Statistics." Working paper of Wyse Advertising.

———. (n.d.,b). "MDPREF–A Tool for Mapping of Perceptual Data." Working paper of Wyse Advertising.

Lawless, Michael W. and Robert J. Fisher. (1990). "Sources of Durable Competitive Advantage in New Products." *Journal of Product Innovation Management,* pp. 35-44.

Levine, Arthur M. (1983). "Does the Home Buyer Need His Own Broker?" *Real Estate Review, XIII* Spring, pp. 98-100.

Levitt, Theodore. (1960). "Marketing Myopia." *Harvard Business Review,* July/August, pp. 45-56.

———. (1976). "The Industrialization of Service." *Harvard Business Review,* September/October, pp. 63-74.

Levy, Diane and Carol Suprenant. (1982). "A Comparison of Responses to Dissatisfaction with Products and Services." In H. Keith Hunt and Ralph L. Day (eds.), *Conceptual and Empirical Contributions to Consumer Satisfaction and Complaining Behavior.* Bloomington, IN: Indiana University Press, pp. 43-49.

Locus, Inc. (1984). "Proforma Financial Statements."

Marketing News. (1992). "Study: Launching New Products Is Worth the Risk." January 20, p. 2.

———. (1994). "Standard Farm Fare Sells In New Package." January 31, p. 6.

Marquis, Donald G. (1976). "The Anatomy of Successful Innovations." In Robert R. Rothberg (ed.), *Corporate Strategy and Product Innovation.* New York: The Free Press, pp. 14-25.

McCarthy, Kevin F. (1979). "Housing Search and Mobility." Santa Monica, CA: Rand Corporation.

McKitterick, John B. (1957). "What is the Marketing Management Concept?" In Frank M. Bass (ed.), *The Frontiers of Marketing Thought and Action.* Chicago: American Marketing Association, pp. 71-82.

Meyer, Marshall W. and Lynne G. Zucker. (1989). *Permanently Failing Organizations.* Newbury Park, CA: Sage.

Miller, Cyndie. (1994). "Dental Insurer Offers Absolute Guarantee on Its Services." *Marketing News,* March 14, pp. 8, 18.

Miller, Michael W. (1987). "At Many Firms, Employees Speak a Language That's All Their Own." *The Wall Street Journal,* December 29, p. 15.

Monroe, Kent B. (1993). "Pricing Practices Which Endanger Profits." *Pricing Strategy & Practice.* Volume 1, No. 1, pp. 4-10.

Morris, Michael and William Lundstrom. (1984). "Product Innovation and the Strategic Impact of the Marketing Concept." In Russell W. Belk, Robert Peterson, Gerald S. Albaun, Morris B. Holbrook, Roger A. Kerin, Naresh K. Malhotra, and Peter Wright (eds.), *1984 AMA Educators' Proceedings.* Chicago: American Marketing Association, pp. 226-230.

National Association of Realtors. (1989). "Media Kit."

National Market Measures. (1985a). "Qualitative Research Results for *Locus.*"

_____. (1985b). "Research Results for *Locus.*"

_____. (1988). "Qualitative Research Results for Home Characterizations."

_____. (1989). "Qualitative Research Results for *AutoAd*: A Computerized Car Advertisement Program."

Newspaper Advertising Bureau. (1986). "Real Estate Classified: A Study of Prospect Status, Readership & Interest."

Pacanowsky, Michael E. and Nick O'Donnell-Trujillo. (1983). "Organizational Communication as Cultural Performance." *Communication Monographs,* June, pp. 126-147.

Pearson, Andrall E. (1988). "Tough-Minded Ways to Get Innovative." *Harvard Business Review,* May-June, pp. 99-106.

Peters, Thomas and Robert Waterman. (1982). *In Search of Excellence.* New York: Harper & Row.

Reason, Peter. (1994). "Three Approaches to Participative Inquiry." In Norman K. Denzin and Yvonna S. Lincoln (eds.), *Handbook of Qualitative Research.* Thousand Oaks, CA: Sage, pp. 324-339.

Robertson, Thomas S. and Hubert Gatignon. (1987). "The Diffusion of High Technology Innovation: A Marketing Perspective." In Johannes M. Pennings and Arend Buitendam (eds.), *New Technology as Organizational Innovation.* Cambridge, MA: Ballinger, pp. 179-197.

Robinson, William T. and Claes Fornell. (1985). "Sources of Market Pioneer Advantages in Consumer Goods Industries." *Journal of Marketing Research,* pp. 305-317.

Rogers, Everett M. (1983). *Diffusion of Innovation,* 3rd edition. New York: The Free Press.

Ronstadt, Robert. (1988). "The Corridor Principle." *Journal of Business Venturing,* pp. 31-40.

Ross, Jerry and Barry M. Staw. (1986). "Expo '86: An Escalation Prototype." *Administrative Science Quarterly,* Vol. 31, pp. 274-297.

Ross, Jerry and Barry M. Staw. (1993). "Organizational Escalation and Exit: Lessons from the Shoreham Nuclear Power Plant." *Academy of Management Journal,* pp. 701-732.

Scheuing, Eberhard E. and Eugene M. Johnson. (1987). "New Product Management in Service Industries: An Early Assessment." In Carol Suprenant (ed.), *Add Value to Your Service.* Chicago: American Marketing Association, pp. 91-95.

Shanks, Donald. (1985). "Profit-Oriented Customer Service." Presentation at "Markets . . . The Moving Target," sponsored by *Sales & Marketing Management* magazine. Chicago, IL, June 12.

Shugan, Steven M. (1987). "Establishing Brand Positioning Maps Using Supermarket Scanning Data." *Journal of Marketing Research,* February, pp. 1-18.

Sisodia, Rajendra S. (1993). "The 'Ideal' Brokerage Firm: Revealed Structure and Symetries in the Institutional Equity Services Market." *Journal of Professional Services Marketing,* Volume 10, No. 1, pp. 119-145.

Stacey, Ralph D. (1992). *Managing the Unknowable: Strategic Boundaries Between Order and Chaos in Organizations.* San Francisco: Jossey-Bass.

Staw, Barry M. (1976). "Knee Deep in the Big Muddy: A Study of Escalating Commitment to a Chosen Course of Action." *Organizational Behavior and Human Performance,* p. 27.

———— and Jerry Ross. (1987a). "Understanding Escalation Situations: Antecedents, Prototypes, and Solutions." In L. L. Cummings and Barry M. Staw (eds.), *Research in Organizational Behavior,* Greenwich, CT: JAI Press.

———— . (1987b). "Knowing When to Pull the Plug." *Harvard Business Review,* March-April, pp. 68-74.

Stell, Roxanne and Raymond P. Fisk. (1986). "Services Images: A Synthesis of Image Creation and Management." In M. Venkatesan, Diane M. Schmalensee, and Claudia Marshall (eds.), *Creativity in Services Marketing: What's New, What Works, What's Developing*. Chicago: American Marketing Association, pp. 113-117.

Stern, Barbara B. (1988). "Figurative Language in Services Advertising: The Nature and Uses of Imagery." In Michael J. Houston, (ed.), *Advances in Consumer Research, Vol. XV*. Provo, UT: Association for Consumer Research, pp. 185-190.

Susbauer, Jeffrey C., Dennis J. Cahill, Robert M. Warshawsky, and James Beckman. (1994). "Culture Consulting in a Family-Owned Business." Paper presented at the Small Business Institute Directors Association Annaul Meeting, February.

Taylor, James W. (1977). "A Striking Characteristic of Innovations." *Journal of Marketing Research*, February, pp. 104-107.

Trombetta, William L. (1980). "Using Antitrust Law to Control Anticompetitive Real Estate Industry Practices." *Journal of Consumer Affairs*, pp. 142-155.

Twain, Mark. (1889). *A Connecticut Yankee in King Arthur's Court*. New York: Charles L. Webster & Co.

United States Department of Commerce, International Trade Administration. (1983). An Assessment of United States Competitiveness in High Technology Industries. Washington, DC: Government Printing Office.

Verba, Steven M. and Dennis J. Cahill. (1993). "Interactivity: The Successful Semiotics of a Product Failure." In *Proceedings of the Third Biennial High Technology Management Conference*. Boulder, CO: University of Colorado, pp. 377-383.

Von Hippel, Eric. (1986). "Lead Users: A Source of Novel Product Concepts." *Management Science*, pp. 791-805.

Voss, Christopher A. (1985a). "The Role of Users in the Development of Applications Software." *Journal of Product Innovation Management*, pp. 113-121.

_____. (1985b). "Determinants of Success in the Development of Applications Software." *Journal of Product Innovation Management*, pp. 122-129.

Wallace, Janet D. (1984). "Memo," (about realtors).

———— . (1985). "Memo," (about DECOY, Inc.'s Touchscreen system).

Webster's New World Dictionary of the American Language. (1984). Cleveland, OH: The World Publishing Company.

Wiesendanger, Betsy. (1991). "Kiosks: Automated Wonder or Lead Balloon?" *Sales and Marketing Management,* August, pp. 40-43.

Zoslov, Pamela. (1992). "The Paper Chase: How the *Edition* died, the *Free Times* was born and Bill Gunlocke is Coping." *Cleveland Magazine,* November, pp. 60-62.

Index

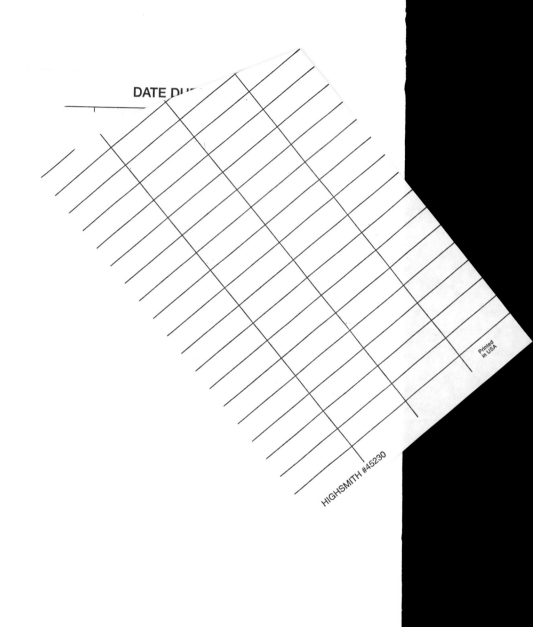

DATE DUE

HIGHSMITH #45230

Printed in USA